FORMULAS OF THE MORAL LAW

Allen Wood
Indiana University
Stanford University (emeritus)

ELEMENTS IN THE PHILOSOPHY OF IMMANUEL KANT

Cambridge Elements ⸗

CAMBRIDGE
UNIVERSITY PRESS

University Printing House, Cambridge CB2 8BS, United Kingdom

One Liberty Plaza, 20th Floor, New York, NY 10006, USA

477 Williamstown Road, Port Melbourne, VIC 3207, Australia

4843/24, 2nd Floor, Ansari Road, Daryaganj, Delhi – 110002, India

79 Anson Road, #06–04/06, Singapore 079906

Cambridge University Press is part of the University of Cambridge.

It furthers the University's mission by disseminating knowledge in the pursuit of education, learning, and research at the highest international levels of excellence.

www.cambridge.org
Information on this title: www.cambridge.org/9781108413176
DOI: 10.1017/9781108332736

First published 2017

A catalogue record for this publication is available from the British Library.

ISBN 978-1-108-41317-6 Paperback
978-1-108-41317-6 PB
978-1-10833273-6 OC
978-1-108-33274-3 RE
ISSN 2397-9461

Formulas of the Moral Law

Allen Wood

Abstract: *This Element defends a reading of Kant's formulas of the moral law in* Groundwork for the Metaphysics of Morals. *It disputes a long tradition accepted both by Kant's critics and defenders, concerning what the first formula (Universal Law/Law of Nature) attempts to do. But the reading proposed here is the only one that agrees with both what Kant says about these formulas and with what he actually does with them in his discussion of the four famous examples – which are also discussed here at some length. The Element also expounds the Formulas of Humanity, Autonomy and the Realm of Ends, arguing that it is only the Formula of Humanity from which Kant derives general duties, and that it is only the third formula (Autonomy/Realm of Ends) that represents a complete and definitive statement of the moral principle as Kant derives it in the* Groundwork. *The Element also disputes the common claim that the various formulas are "equivalent," arguing that this claim is either false or else nonsensical because grounded on a false premise about what Kant thinks a moral principle is for.*

Keywords: *Kant's ethics, categorical imperative, formula of the moral law, universal law, humanity as end in itself, autonomy*

9781108413176 PB, 9781108332736 OC, 9781108332743 RE

Kant's ethical theory has traditionally been received, both by its sympathizers and its critics, largely through his short treatise *Groundwork for the Metaphysics of Morals* (1785). In the *Groundwork*, Kant formulates the supreme principle of morality in a number of different ways. Most prominent in the reception of his theory has been his first formulation: the Formula of

Universal Law (FUL). From the beginning, both the interpretation of this formula and its purpose in moral reasoning have been controversial. I believe they have also been generally misunderstood.

The resurgence of interest in Kant's ethics in the late twentieth century was led by John Rawls and Onora O'Neill, who identified FUL with "the Categorical Imperative," and interpreted it as a strict "CI-Procedure" providing a general discursive criterion of moral right and wrong (O'Neill, 2013 [1975], Chapter 2; cf. Rawls, 1989, 2000, pp. 162–181). From the start, however, Kant's critics – beginning with Gottlob August Tittel (1739–1816) (Tittel, 2012 [1786]) and later such famous philosophers as Hegel, Mill, and Sidgwick – questioned whether FUL can provide any such procedural criterion of right and wrong. I do not pretend to know the best interpretation of FUL when it is read with these aims. Nor do I know whether, so interpreted, it could successfully provide a general moral criterion or procedure – though I doubt it. What I am certain of is that both sides in this dispute are misreading *Kant*. This essay aims to explain Kant's actual use of this and the *Groundwork*'s other formulas of the moral law.

First Part: The System of Formulas

§1. *The Aims of the* Groundwork

It took Kant a long time to formulate his mature moral theory. By the mid-1760s, after a flirtation with Hutcheson's moral sense theory, Kant decided to reject feeling as the foundation of ethics and identify his position with the phrase 'metaphysics of morals.' By this he meant that he took the foundations of ethics to lie in what he called 'metaphysics' – that is, *synthetic a priori cognitions from concepts*. It was not until nearly twenty years later that he published even the first, cautious 'laying of the foundations' (*Grundlegung*) for a metaphysics of morals (1785). The aims of Kant's little book were very limited: "a search for and establishment of the supreme principle of morality" (G 4:392). The *search* occupies the first two sections, and the *establishment* (or "deduction") of the principle occurs only in the Third Section. A fuller presentation of Kant's system of duties had to wait until the very end of his career: the *Metaphysics of Morals* (1798).

Kant's search for the supreme principle of morality. The first section of the *Groundwork* derives a formula of the moral law from the presuppositions of "common rational moral cognition" (G 4:393). This phrase denotes the knowledge of moral truth that Kant takes the ordinary moral agent to possess and to display in everyday judgments, feelings, and actions when these conform to morality. Kant elicits this everyday cognition in the form of our anticipated assent to certain propositions about what it is that we most value as moral agents, and of the kind of value that we regard as most central to morality itself. Kant expects us to assent to the claim that nothing is good without limitation except a good will (G 4:393–396), and that what is central to morality is a special case of the good will – the case where someone must act with self-constraint on moral grounds. Then the action is not merely "in conformity with duty" (*pflichtmäßig*) but also "from duty" (*aus Pflicht*) (G 4:397–399). This constraint exhibits awareness of an obligating rational law that is universally valid for all rational agents (G 4:401). That thought leads to Kant's first formulation of the moral principle, the Formula of Universal Law (or FUL): "I ought never to conduct myself except so *that I could also will that my maxim become a universal law*" (G 4:402). This is the only formula developed out of common rational moral cognition; it is therefore apparently the only formula we need to employ in everyday life. Even it, however, is not thought by the ordinary moral agent in this abstract form, but is an implicit standard of moral judgment (G 4:403).

Kant undertakes a fuller search for the supreme principle of morality in the Second Section, based on a properly *philosophical* investigation of the principles of rational volition (G 4:412). Kant distinguishes three such standards. The *first* is that of instrumental or *technical* reason: that we rationally should constrain ourselves to take the necessary means to an end we have adopted at our discretion (G 4:415). The *second* is that of prudential or *pragmatic* reason: that we rationally should form the idea of a sum-total of achievable satisfactions of our empirical desires or inclinations (under the name of 'welfare' or 'happiness'), and rationally should give the pursuit of this end priority over any other ends of inclination with which it might conflict (G 4:416). The *third* is that of *moral* reason, which commands us unconditionally to do or omit certain actions, and to set certain ends, irrespective of any ends or desires we may have that are extrinsic to the moral command (G 4:416).

Kant represents these rational standards in the form of *imperatives*. This term does not refer to a *grammatical* form, but instead to a ground or reason for rational self-constraint. Kant distinguishes *hypothetical* imperatives, grounded on an independently adopted end, from *categorical* imperatives, which presuppose no independently given end as a condition of their rational validity. The instrumental imperative and the imperative of prudence are both *hypothetical*: the former is grounded on some end we have set arbitrarily or at our discretion; the latter on the end of happiness, which every finite rational agent does set. The rational validity of hypothetical imperatives, Kant argues, is *analytic* – that is, it is grounded solely on the content of the mere concept of the imperative itself. More specifically, it is contained in the very concept of *setting an end* that insofar as one's actions are governed by that end, one rationally *ought* to take the necessary means to it. Of course specific technical rules and counsels of prudence are not analytic; they are not even practical propositions, but typically contingent and empirical *theoretical* truths (FI 20:197–200). The rational self-constraint of hypothetical imperatives, however, is grounded analytically on the very *concept* of setting an end, which includes in it the normative requirement that we should take the necessary means to the end we have set.

Categorical imperatives, however, are not analytic. Even their possibility will have to be established. Kant does this only in the Third Section, where a deduction of the moral law is to be provided. Until this happens, as Kant reminds us repeatedly (even obsessively) in the First and Second Sections, we must regard the whole of morality as possibly an illusion or figment of the brain (G 4:394, 404, 407, 419–420, 423, 425, 429, 431, 445).

Kant calls the three (or five) statements of the moral law, *formulas* of the categorical imperative. In a later work he says he means this term in the sense mathematicians use it. A 'formula' is something that "determines quite precisely what must be done to solve a problem" (CPrR 5:8 n). Each formula addresses a different problem. We will see in due course what each of the specific problems is, and we must be careful not to make hasty assumptions about what Kant thinks a moral principle is *for*.

Kant's search for the moral principle, as we learn after the three main formulas of the moral law have been presented, is intended to be systematic (see Wood, 2001). It is organized according to a triad drawn from Kant's theory of concepts, when that theory is applied to the concept of a practical principle or maxim (G 4:436). A maxim is a subjective norm imposed by a rational agent on its actions (G 4:421, cf. CPrR 5:19). It is something like an *intention*, if we think of intentions as subjective norms we impose on our actions. A maxim, however, would not be the intention of a particular action at a particular time and place, but rather a *generalized* intention: to do a certain kind of action whenever certain specifiable conditions obtain. A maxim is therefore a subjective norm – one we impose on ourselves at our discretion. A maxim typically has a *form*: the *kind* of action; also a *matter*: an end for the sake of which the subject acts. According to Kant's theory of concepts, the complete concept of an individual always involves a *complete determination* of the individual in respect of its properties. In the case of the formulas, this refers to the *complete formula*, in which form and matter have been combined (G 4:436).

The first and third formulas, though not the second, have both a more abstract and a more "intuitive" variant. The latter variants are said by Kant to be "closer to intuition" and hence "nearer to feeling," and therefore better able to help the moral principle gain "access" or "entry" (*Eingang*) to human beings through intuition and feeling (G 4:389, 405, 409, 436–437). The intuitive variant of the first formula adds to the abstract idea of universal law the more concrete thought of a possible *nature* as embodying a *system of laws*. The intuitive variant of the third formula adds to the idea of rational will regarded as legislating universally the more concrete thought of an entire *community* of rational beings, and the *shared system of their collective ends* that would result from the perfect obedience to such a universal legislation.

The entire system of these formulas is this:

First formula

FUL   *Formula of Universal Law*: "Act only in accordance with that maxim through which you at the same time can will that it become a universal law" (G 4:421),

with its more intuitive variant,

FLN   *Formula of the Law of Nature*: "So act, as if the maxim of your action were to become through your will a **universal law of nature**" (G 4:421).

Second formula

FH   *Formula of Humanity as End in Itself*: "So act that you use humanity, as much in your own person as in the person of every other, always at the same time as an end and never merely as a means" (G 4:429).

Third formula

FA   *Formula of Autonomy*: "the idea of the will of every rational being as a will giving universal law" (G 4:431; cf. 4:432), or "Not to choose otherwise than so that the maxims of one's choice are at the same time comprehended with it in the same volition as universal law" (G 4:440; cf. 4:432, 434, 438),

with its more intuitive variant,

FRE   *Formula of the Realm of Ends*: "Act in accordance with maxims of a universally legislative member for a merely possible realm of ends" (G 4:439; cf. 4:433, 437–439).

Each of the formulas is derived from the very concept of a categorical imperative: the first from its form, the second from its matter; the third combines the first formula with the second. The first two formulas are thus in a sense one-sided (form without matter, matter without form). The form of law, Kant says, is the law considered objectively (in terms of its universal obligation), while the matter is the law considered subjectively (in terms of the rational ground or motive for the subject's obedience to it). The third formula, FA (or its variant, FRE), combines the first two formulas (G 4:431). It is this *complete determination* form of the law that is later used in the *deduction* (G 4:446–455). It is also FA that is used as the definitive statement of the moral law in Kant's later ethical works: the *Critique of Practical Reason* (CPrR 5:30) and the *Metaphysics of Morals* (MM 6:225–226).

Kant also proposes to systematize his presentation of the three formulas according to his categories of quantity: *unity, plurality, totality* (G 4:436). In Kant's table of categories, the category of unity corresponds to the universal form of judgment (*All* S is P); the category of plurality corresponds to the particular form (*Some* S is P); and the category of totality corresponds to the singular form (*The* S is P – representing the singular or completely determined concept of an individual thing) (CPR A70/B95, A80/B106). FUL/FLN thus represents the universal form of moral laws, FH the plurality of particular ends in themselves that are the matter of the law; likewise, FA/FRE results from combining FUL/FLN with FH. FA/FRE thus neither requires nor receives any grounding except from the way it combines FUL/FLN and FH. FA/FRE is the *complete* presentation of the supreme principle of morality.

§2. Derivation of the Formulas from the Concept of a Categorical Imperative

This is not an essay about Kant's *derivation* of his formulas, but about the formulas themselves – what they mean, and the specific problems they are meant to solve. But the meaning of any philosophical thesis is determined by the arguments for it, so I need to introduce the formulas by saying something briefly about the way Kant proposes to derive each from the mere concept of a categorical imperative.

Universal law. A categorical imperative is a principle that rationally constrains any moral agent irrespective of any contingent desires or discretionary ends the agent may have. It therefore applies to all rational agents universally and in the same way. From this point of view, therefore, the only content thought in the concept of such an imperative is conformity of the will to the idea of universal legislation itself – to those principles by which all rational beings might rationally will to constrain themselves and all others (G 4:402). We should note that this requirement of universal validity is not for Kant a specifically *moral* or *ethical* requirement at all. That's what it means to say that it is purely *formal*. It expresses only the minimal standard of all rationality, whether theoretical, practical, or even aesthetic. The concept of an objectively valid judgment is simply one that is valid universally for all rational beings (P 4:298). Thus it is a rational constraint on all thinking that we ought to accept only that whose ground or rule of acceptance could be made a universal principle for the use of reason (WOT 8:146 n). Even a correct judgment of taste is one considered universally valid (CJ 5:283–284). An action is right (not ethically, but merely in the sense required for everyone's external freedom) if it or its maxim are consistent with the freedom of all according to universal law (MM 6:230).

Humanity as end in itself. The mere *form* of a categorical imperative, therefore, is not sufficient to get us to a genuine metaphysics of *morals*. For that we need not only the *form* but also the *matter* of a categorical imperative, namely the way it is "bound up (fully *a priori*) with the concept of the will of a rational being in general." By this Kant means: the rational ground that would motivate obedience to a categorical imperative. It is to obtain the concept of such a ground that we must "take one step beyond, namely to a metaphysics [of morals]" (G 4:426–427). In other words, we have not reached the principle for which we are searching in the *Groundwork* until we have derived not only FUL/FLN but also FH.

Some philosophers have thought that practical rationality consists solely in choosing the correct instrumental means to ends given by desire independently of reason. They have therefore sometimes denied that there could be any ground for obedience to a Kantian categorical imperative. Kant's direct response to their objections is his derivation of FH. The ground of obedience to a categorical imperative, he argues, must be an *end*, but end must be necessarily connected with the concept of a rational will and equally valid for all rational beings. That is, it must be an end which is *objective* rather than subjective: an end that rationally binds us not because we have set it at our discretion, but because it is necessarily binding on us simply as rational beings. Therefore, it also cannot be some possible *effect* of our actions, since such an effect is regarded as an end only because we have set it as an end at our discretion (G 4:427). The end in question, Kant argues, must be something whose *existence* itself has absolute worth. Kant calls this an "independent" or "self-sufficient" end, and an end having *objective* worth (G 4:427, cf. 4:437). The concept of such an end is what Kant calls an "end in itself" (*Zweck an sich selbst*) (G 4:428).

What could be such an end? In three successive paragraphs, Kant first *supposes*, then *asserts*, and then finally *argues*, that *the end in itself is humanity or rational nature in persons* (G 4:428–429). In this context, 'humanity' does not refer to the special empirical nature of human beings. It refers to the capacity to set ends according to reason (Rel 6:26–27). This includes the *technical* predisposition to choose or invent means to the ends a rational being freely sets, and also the *pragmatic* disposition to combine these ends into an idea of one's welfare or happiness. Thus the concept of *humanity* is distinct from and does not include the concept of *personality* or the moral predisposition (Rel 6:26 n). But Kant argues that any being having humanity also necessarily has personality (Anth 7:322–324; cf. CB 8:111–115). Of course it is a contingent, empirical fact that there exist any beings with such predispositions and capacities. But it is true *a priori* that the rational nature of any such being must be an end in itself.

Kant's argument that humanity is the sole end in itself is brief and notoriously controversial. (My own attempts to interpret the argument can be found at Wood, 1999, pp. 118–139, 2008, pp. 85–93, and

Schönecker and Wood, 2015, pp. 142–149.) For our present purposes, I will present it this way: A categorical imperative, by its
concept, cannot be based on anything regarded as valued contin-
gently or based on the desires or discretionary ends of any rational
agent. Once these ends are excluded, there is no conceivable value
remaining on which it could be based except that of rational agency
itself: specifically, that of the rational beings who are supposed to
have this ground for obeying a categorical imperative. Kant thinks
that in exercising rational agency we implicitly represent ourselves
as having such a value. This is what Kant means by the crucial
premise in his argument for FH: "The human being necessarily
represents his own existence [as an existing end in itself]" (G 4:429).

A natural objection is that there seem to be people who do not do
this. Some people regard themselves as worthless and their existence
as having no value. But this objection fails because it misunderstands
the claim being made. That claim is not one about how people
actually think of their existence. The crucial word 'necessarily'
means that this is a way we *must* represent ourselves in exercising
any rational agency at all – even if we also (incoherently) represent
ourselves and our existence as worthless. The essence of Kant's
argument was later put in an arresting form by Nietzsche: "He who
despises himself still esteems the despiser within himself" (Nietzsche,
2002, Part Four, §78). Kant would understand this not as an empirical
psychological claim, but a *philosophical* one about what we
presuppose in exercising any form of rational agency. In setting any
end, choosing any action, esteeming or despising anything, even
ourselves – we thereby claim authority over our own volitions. We
presuppose a worth that belongs to ourselves, our volition, even an
objective worth which, necessarily and *a priori*, occupies a fundamental place in any system of valuation we might ever adopt on the
basis of our volitions. Philosophies, religions, and neuroses that deny
humanity this worth may be psychologically, socially, and historically
powerful and persistent, but they are always rationally self-
undermining. The pathology, lies, and self-deceptions involved in
them are usually more social than individual. The way out of these
is the long, difficult, and problematic and still incomplete historical

struggle that Kant calls "enlightenment" (*Aufklärung*) (WIE 8:35–42). Kant's moral philosophy was devised for an age of enlightenment.

The first premise of Kant's argument, then, is that no rational being can coherently fail to represent its own existence as an end in itself. But FH commands us to regard humanity or rational nature as an end in itself in *all* rational beings. In a footnote, Kant notes that this extension cannot be grounded on the premise he has stated, so it must for the moment remain only a "postulate"; the grounds for it will be presented in the Third Section (G 4:429 n). The argument there is that positive freedom, the capacity for self-legislation, must be ascribed to all rational beings (G 4:448). The argument of the *Groundwork*, therefore, circles back on itself – though the circle is not vicious. It's merely that the ground of the *deduction* of the moral law – the unprovable yet unavoidable pre-supposition that our will is free – also plays an indispensable role in developing the *matter* of the law: humanity as end in itself.

The claim that humanity or rational nature in persons is an end itself applies equally to good people and to bad people. The kind of *value* it attributes to persons is not a claim that all persons are "good people" (by a moral standard or any other). What sort of claim is it? A provisional answer is that it says we, and all others, must always be considered fundamentally as co-participants in human delibera-tions, co-choosers – never merely objects to be manipulated, pushed around, or merely causally influenced by others, even for what these (paternalistic) deliberators consider to be the "good" of those cho-sen for. This is what Kant is saying in the opening sentences of the *Anthropology*, where he boldly distinguishes human persons from everything else in nature on the ground that a person alone can say 'I' and therefore must not be treated only as an object or a thing (Anth 7:127). Treating others as ends in themselves has other con-sequences as well, which we will explore provisionally in §7.

Autonomy. FA/FRE is not based on any independent argument from the concept of a categorical imperative. Instead it is grounded on the combination of the ideas contained in the two (one-sided: formal, then material) formulas, FUL and FH. "The ground of a practical legislation, namely, lies *objectively in the rule*, namely the form of universality (in accordance with the first principle), but *subjectively* it lies in the *end*; but the subject of all ends is every rational being as end in itself (in accordance with the second principle); from this now follows the third practical principle of the will . . . the idea *of the will of every rational being as a will giving universal law*" (G 4:431). Kant does not mean that we can validly infer FA from the formal statements of FUL and FH simply by the rules of formal logic. His argument is rather this: The concept of a categorical imperative, or a practical law, contains not only the thought that the law is universally valid, but also the thought that it might be regarded as legislated by a will. What will? Answer: Based on FH, that will that has just been identified as having objective worth as an end in itself.

FA does *not* claim that the authority of the moral law over the rational will is one *conferred* on it by any actual volition (whether divine or human, whether our own will or that of another). Elsewhere Kant distinguishes two species of practical or normative laws: *natural* laws and *positive* (or *statutory*) laws (MM 6:227). It is only *positive* laws that have a specific will as their author and the command of a legislator as the incentive for obedience to them (L-Eth 27:261–262). Natural laws, however, are valid in themselves and "belong to the nature (or essence) of things" (L-Eth 27: 273, 528–529, 29:633–634; cf. Rel 6:103–104). Literally speaking, they have neither an author nor a legislator. The moral law is a natural law, not a positive law, so it has neither an author nor a legislator. Kant's principle of autonomy is based on the thought that although the moral law has neither an author nor a legislator, we may nevertheless *regard* the idea of every rational will as the legislator of the moral law and *consider* our own rational will as its author (G 4:431). The word 'idea' is essential to this first formulation of FA. An *idea* is a pure concept of reason to which no empirical instance (in this case no finite human will) can ever be adequate (CPR A312–319/B368–375). It is the *idea* of the will, not our own fallible and finite wills, which we *regard* as the legislator and *consider* as the author of the moral law. Thus only the will that in fact obeys the law obeys only its own rational will, and can be regarded as having legislated the law it obeys. Any will that does not obey the moral law is not fully autonomous, even if it has the capacity for autonomy; for it, the authority of the law depends only on the law's rational validity in itself. (I discuss these matters at greater length in Wood, 2008, Chapter 6.)

Second Part: Universal Law

§3. *What is a Moral Principle* For?

Before we begin our discussion of FUL/FLN, it will help to make explicit some of the presuppositions readers may bring to the *Groundwork* that are likely to lead to misreadings. They go something like this: We take for granted that a *moral principle* is a rational procedure which, when brought to bear on a set of facts, provides us with a criterion enabling us to distinguish right actions from wrong ones. Such a principle might be regarded as something like a function taking us from a theoretical input (a set of factual assertions) to a practical output (a decision about what to do or at least an ordered set of preferences). Alternatively, we tacitly assume that a moral principle must be a criterion enabling us to say which actions, given morally neutral descriptions, are right and which wrong, which permissible and which impermissible, or else a procedure of discursive reasoning that justifies such judgments.

One obvious model for a *moral principle* in this sense is utilitarian: The input is a set of utility functions of those whose interests are in question, together with a set of causal claims about the likely effects of various actions open to us on the satisfaction of these utility functions. The output is a choice, or a preference-ordering among the available actions, namely that choice or ordering which maximizes utility. Different forms of utilitarianism offer us different functions. Some focus on acts, some on rules, some on moral codes. (An important contribution to thinking about this variety was Lyons, 1965.) The utilitarian model so dominated Anglophone ethics until well after the mid-twentieth century, that analytical philosophers had mostly turned their attention away from normative ethics and toward meta-ethics – and toward an anti-realist meta-ethics at that. But by the late twentieth century, other philosophers had begun to worry that utilitarianism leaves too many things out. They thought that moral philosophy is not, as moral psychologist Joshua Greene apparently wishes it were, merely a matter of engaging the "cognitive" part of our brain – the part that makes "cost–benefit" calculations – and suppressing the "emotional" parts of the brain, whose misguided deontological instincts might interfere with cold, intellectual reckonings directed at calculating good and bad consequences (Greene, 2008). The non-utilitarian moral philosophers began to wonder: Can utilitarian principles take proper account of the difference between persons? Can they accommodate individual rights and justice? Can they explain why some ethical questions seem to be matters of principle that might even override the production of the best outcomes? For these malcontents, Kant seemed to offer a better kind of procedural calculation. Late twentieth-century (neo-) Kantians therefore offered a rigorous four-step "CI-Procedure," based (as they thought) on FUL (or more precisely, on its intuitive variant, FLN). This procedure was most fully expounded in O'Neill (2013[1975]), but also succinctly presented in Rawls (1989):

1. First step: Formulate a maxim: a way you have acted, or are considering acting.
2. Second step: Generalize it, so that it represents a way of acting that everyone might adopt.
3. Third step: Expand the generalized maxim into a possible world (or a possible nature, sometimes called a "perturbed social world") in which the actual world is modified by supposing that everyone follows the generalized maxim.
4. Fourth step: Determine whether you can will to be a member of the world so represented. If you can, then the maxim is permissible; if not, it is impermissible.

As a matter of intellectual history, it is unlikely that Kant could have made his way back into Anglophone ethics in any other way. To be taken seriously, Kantians had to provide their own distinctive answers to the questions: *What should we do, by what intellectual procedure should we decide what to do, and by what reasoning should we justify our decisions?* The thing to notice, however, is that it was being taken for granted on all sides that moral philosophy is concerned solely with solving *intellectual* problems about the rational procedures to be used in making decisions and justifying them. That's what a moral principle has to be *for*. In Kant's day too this was the dominant approach, the one taken by the Wolffian school in which Kant was educated. Wolffian answers were perfectionist rather than utilitarian or (neo-) Kantian, but they involved the same basic notion of what a moral principle is *for*.[1]

It has not been sufficiently appreciated how radically Kant rejected this entire tradition. Under the influence of that most subversive of all eighteenth-century moralists, Jean-Jacques Rousseau, Kant came up with an entirely different conception of what a moral principle is *for*.

To get an idea of Kant's alternative, consider this 1975 *New Yorker* cartoon by Dana Fradon:

"Miss Dugan, will you send someone in here who can distinguish right from wrong?"

---

[1] The Wolffians held that monarchs and ministers need enlightened philosophers to tell them what to do. The background assumption was the same as in utilitarianism: Philosophers (social engineers) can do a better job of telling other people how to live than these people could figure out for themselves. This was the direction in which Wolff's philosophy was especially taken by the Enlightenment sect known as the 'cameralists,' led by J. H. Justi (1717-1768). For a good account of cameralism and Kant's rejection of it see Kaufman (1996, Chapter 2).

This group of middle-aged men in suits and ties might be executives of a corporation in mid-town Manhattan. Having spent half a century hanging around universities, however, the sentimental romantic in me prefers to think of it as an ethically compromised ethics committee at a prestigious university. Whoever these pompous little men are, they have a decision to make about some sticky business. They are asking a secretary to send out for advice. At the risk of spoiling the joke, I will first describe what *seems* to be going on, then say what is *really* going on. The joke lies in the discrepancy between the two.

The chairman of the group is apparently asking for someone with the appropriate expertise. If Miss Dugan took an ethics course in college, she might go out and get the moral philosopher who taught it. If Miss Dugan got a utilitarian, the little men might (or they might not) get different advice from what they'd get from a (neo-) Kantian with a four-step CI-Procedure. Or if the ethics professor went back to the basics of more recent moral philosophy, appealing to "our" intuitions about how to handle lifeboat shortages and runaway trolleys, then the committee might be told precisely under what conditions anyone whose hand happens to be on the lever of death may without qualm deliberately choose to kill innocent people in the name of some greater good. But one thing is clear: the expert advice would consist in the answers to intellectual questions about what people should do and what discursive reasoning would justify their decisions. That's the professor's area of expertise. That's what moral principles are *for*.

This is what *seems to be going on* in the cartoon. But if you get the joke, you see that it's not what is really going on at all. If Miss Dugan sent out for a moral philosopher who offers this kind of advice, then she would not have gotten the joke. For the bewildered committee, at least, already knows that this kind of advice is not what they really need – even if officially, on the surface, it seems to be what they are asking for. If, on the other hand, Miss Dugan had gotten the joke – and if he had been available – she might have gone out and gotten the author of the *Groundwork*. Kant may have no great reputation for a sense of humor, but *he* would have gotten the joke.

The joke (in case *you* don't get it) depends on seeing that "distinguishing right from wrong" is *not a matter of intellectual expertise*. As far as that goes, these poor guys already know right from wrong. They are about to do something they *know* is wrong. Yet they are tempted to do it anyway, no doubt on the ground that doing it serves "the greater good" (the firm's, the university's, or just their own). They are in a quandary because they are tempted to think that this "greater good" might justify (perhaps only "just this once") their doing what – with the "deontic" (that is, the morally decent) part of their brains – they *know perfectly well* is wrong. The call to Miss Dugan is an admission that, in their condition of moral weakness, the shallow "cognitive" (i.e. the " cost–benefit" or "greater good") part of their brains has so disoriented their good judgment that they no longer know what they know and what they don't. But at least they do know that they no longer know what they know; that last pitiful shred of human decency shows itself in their desperate plea for help, comically masquerading as a dignified professional request for outside expertise.

What they lack is not intellectual expertise but moral *character* – and consequently, uncorrupted *judgment*. What they need is not professional advice but a *moral compass*. They need to find their way back home to what Kant, in his eighteenth-century scholastic terminology, would call their "common rational moral cognition." That's what's *really* going on in the cartoon. The joke – which, like the humorless Kantian that I am, I have now spoiled for you by explaining it – lies in the incongruity between what *seems* to be going on: the committee's self-important and thoroughly professional request for specialized expertise, and what is *really* going on: their dismal, reluctant confession that they are hopelessly flawed human beings.

Kant sees the situation of the ordinary moral agent in much the same way this cartoon sees the situation of this ethically challenged little quartet; *except* that Kant –Thank goodness! – is not as cynical as the sophisticated cartoonists whose work gets into the *New Yorker*. Kant thinks that all ordinary human beings possess "common rational moral cognition" – the *intellectual* capacity to distinguish right from wrong; and also the moral capacity to *choose* what is right, if only they have the *strength of character* and the *good judgment* to do so. He agrees with the point of the cartoon: that the moral principle ordinary moral agents need is *not* one that provides them with an intellectual procedure or criterion of rightness. It is rather one that would give them the moral *orientation* they sometimes lack. Immediately after introducing FUL in the First Section of the *Groundwork*, Kant declares:

> Thus in the moral cognition of common human reason we have attained to its principle, which it obviously does not think abstractly in such a universal form, but actually has before its eyes and uses as its standard of judgment. It would be easy here to show how, with this compass in hand, it knows its way around very well in all the cases that come before it, how to distinguish what is good, what is evil, what conforms to duty or is contrary to duty, if without teaching it the least new thing, one only makes it aware of its own principle, as Socrates did; and thus that it needs no science and philosophy to know what one has to do in order to be honest and good, or indeed, even wise and virtuous. It might even have been conjectured in advance that the acquaintance with what every human being is obliged to do, hence to know, would be the affair of everyone, even of the most common human being. (G 4:403–404)

If FUL really were a rigorous four-step CI-Procedure for deciding what to do, then it would make no sense for Kant to say that common human reason can make use of it *without needing to think it abstractly in universal form*. For rigorous, ponderous explicit reasoning is precisely what both utilitarians and CI-Proceduralists have to offer as their stock in trade. That's what they were assuming a moral principle has to be *for*. And that's just where Rousseau and Kant disagree with them.

FUL and moral judgment. Kant describes FUL as a "standard of judgment." Later he will call its intuitive variant FLN a "canon of judgment" (G 4:424). In the second Critique, he calls FLN a "typic of pure practical judgment" and a "rule of judgment" (CPrR 5: 67–70). Philosophers nowadays often apply the term 'moral judgment' to many different things, even including the outcome of discursive reasoning and decision procedures. But for Kant, 'judgment' has a much narrower and more specific meaning. It refers to a special capacity of the mind that enables it to *mediate between* a general concept and its particular instances. *Determining* judgment is the skill needed to apply a general concept correctly to particular cases (CPR A132–134/B171–174; cf. Anth 7:199). *Reflecting* judgment is the capacity to go from a particular instance, or a manifold of them, to a suitable concept that enables their manifold to be grasped in one consciousness (FI 20:211, CJ 5: 179–180). The situation of the ordinary moral agent, as Kant thinks of it, is one in which the question is how a moral concept ("good, evil, what conforms to duty, what is contrary to duty") is to be applied to a particular case by means of *determining* judgment.

In the passage quoted above, Kant calls FUL a *compass* – that is, a device for *orienting* ourselves. One of Kant's important theses about the nature of space is that orientation – knowing where one is, where one is going, or the difference between front and back, up and down, right and left – is not ultimately something we could learn by applying an intellectual procedure. It is a matter not for the understanding or discursive reasoning, but for direct perception or even *subjective feeling* (P 4:286, WOT 8:134–135). In morality, orientation is specifically a matter for *judgment*, which Kant considers a matter of *feeling* (G 4:451). A *standard* of judgment does admit of a rational presentation (this is precisely what FUL/FLN are). But judgment does not operate through explicit reasoning. Orientation is matter of knowing *where you are, here and now*. Moral judgment is a matter of how an already recognized moral duty applies to *this* action, *here* and *now*. As a *standard of judgment*, FUL doesn't give you that information, but it saves you from the disorienting effects of your moral weakness and corruption.

Kant's basic thesis about judgment is that *it can never even in principle be reduced to a discursive procedure* or series of inferences using general concepts (CPR A132–134/B171–174; cf. TP 8:275, Anth 7:199). Suppose I am to decide whether what is before me is an instance of the concept C_1. Imagine that I propose to decide this by applying a discursive principle using a mediating concept: *If something is C_2, then it is C_1.* Now the question becomes whether what is before me is an instance of C_2. If I again try to decide this by a process of discursive reasoning, I need another premise: *If something is C_3, then it is C_2.* That puts before me the question whether it is an instance of C_3. Surely you can see where this is going. At least you can if, through your own capacity of determining judgment, you can apply the philosopher's concept 'vicious infinite regress' to an obvious one of its instances. Inferences based on concepts may help me answer my original question, but at some point they necessarily have to give out. At some point, I must simply *judge* whether the particular before me is an instance of *some* specific concept. I get it right, or I get it wrong. That's all there is to it.

Judgment, according to Kant, is a special talent, partly inborn, partly trained or developed through experience and thinking about particular cases, in which concepts are to be applied – especially difficult or problematic cases. In the Doctrine of Virtue, the task of training our moral judgment is assigned to the "Casuistical Questions" woven into Kant's taxonomy of ethical duties (MM 6:411 and *passim*). A "standard of judgment" *can't* be a discursive procedure, such as a felicific calculus or a CI-Procedure. Instead, FUL/FLN, as a compass or standard of judgment, is an aid in the correct application of moral concepts – such as right or wrong, good or bad, duty or some particular duty. However, Kant assigns to FUL/FLN an even narrower task. It is directed to helping us know our way around when faced with a *specific kind* of moral problem – the kind that makes it especially hard for us, as imperfect rational beings (or for the highbrow yet shabby little committee in the cartoon), to distinguish right from wrong. Specifically, it is the problem posed when we are tempted to let the correct application of the concept of some valid moral principle, requirement, or duty be pre-empted by inclination, advantage, or the "greater good" of some entity with which we identify (the firm or its managers, the university or its faculty or administration). That's what happens when we lose our moral *compass*. Regarded as *formulas* – ways of solving a *problem* (CPrR 5:8 n) – the task of FUL/FLN is correcting our judgment when we are faced with that specific kind of moral difficulty.

Suppose I am in a *tight spot* financially – as Kant says, *im Gedränge* – and realize that I can get out of it quickly and easily by borrowing money from a friend and promising to repay it, which, however, I know I won't be able to do – and also have no intention of ever doing (G 4:402–403). I realize, of course, that normally promises obligate you; and that if I do what I am contemplating then I will be betraying my friend's trust. But wait a minute! I'm in this tight spot, don't you see? I *really need* to get out of it. So I wonder: Does the duty not to make a lying promise and betray my friend *really* apply to me in *this* situation? Couldn't my financial emergency excuse me from the duty – in this one (exceptional) case? This is not a problem of discursive practical reasoning but one of moral *orientation* or *judgment*.

The application of FUL and FLN does of course involve certain kinds of reasoning: about universalizability, what can and can't be laws of nature and what you can rationally will. But we've already seen that Kant does not suppose that ordinary agents explicitly go through this reasoning. FUL/FLN offer us instead only a theoretical account of the reasoning agents are implicitly following when they use the standpoint of impartial reason to correct faulty judgment. Kant holds that ordinary agents, when they judge correctly, are guided by these considerations without consciously thinking about them.[2] Even the specific concept of duty to be applied is not made

---

[2] The universalizability tests might be compared (in this respect) to the rules of grammar formulated by linguists, or the complex calculations perceptual psychologists attribute to our visual faculties. To represent Kant as recommending that we go through some explicit "CI-Procedure" in our everyday lives is rather like depicting Noam Chomsky as claiming that we have to go through the rules of transformational grammar before uttering some ordinary English sentence, or David Marr as advocating that we must haul out protractors, measure angles, and do sophisticated geometrical calculations before we can see something that's right in front of us.

fully explicit in Kant's theory until later. The problem FUL
addresses is one that can arise only after reasoning – or "common
rational moral cognition" – has had its say. Kant thinks that ordinary moral agents, in a state of *innocence*, would need nothing at all
from philosophy. The problem is that innocence is fragile – easily
and even inevitably lost, impossible to protect indefinitely, certain
sooner or later to be led astray. For Kant, ordinary agents need
philosophy only because they may be tempted to inflict on themselves what Kant (in his technical terminology) calls a 'dialectic' (or
"logic of illusion," CPR A61/B86, A293/B249). They may apply the
concept of duty deceptively regarding a particular case.

> There is something splendid about innocence, but it is in turn very bad
> that it cannot be protected very well and is easily seduced. On this
> account even wisdom – which consists more in conduct than in knowl-
> edge – also needs science, not in order to learn from it but in order to
> provide entry and durability to its precepts. The human being feels in
> himself a powerful counterweight against all commands of duty ... [in
> the form of] his needs and inclinations ... Now reason commands its
> precepts unremittingly, without promising anything to inclinations,
> thus snubbing and disrespecting, as it were, those impetuous
> claims ... From this arises a *natural dialectic*, that is a propensity to
> ratiocinate against those strict laws of duty, and to bring into doubt
> their validity, or at least their purity and strictness, and where possible,
> to make them better suited to our wishes and inclinations, i.e. at ground
> to corrupt them and deprive them of their entire dignity. (G 4:405)

Perhaps it's worth stressing how consistently Kant carries through
this conception (and no other) of why ordinary moral agents might
need moral philosophy. At the beginning of the Second Section of
the *Groundwork*, Kant berates popular moral philosophy on the
ground of the heterogeneity of the reasons it uses on behalf of
morality "sometimes perfection, sometimes happiness, here
moral feeling, there fear of God, some of this and some of that, all
in a wondrous mixture" (G 4:410). Kant's complaint is that the
many philosophical defenses given for morality are really only so
many opportunities for people to subvert what they already know,

leaving an opening to some sophistical rationale for doing what they know they shouldn't. "By trying to strengthen their medicine in this way, they ruin it." Kant thinks the only way philosophy can really contribute to virtue is by emphasizing the distinctive purity of moral laws and keeping us focused on the moral principle he is in the process of developing in the *Groundwork* (G 4:411 n).

We see the very same thing in other ethical writings. According to the second Critique, the flaw in ethical theories grounded on material principles is not an intellectual flaw but a *moral* flaw (CPrR 5:21–26). In his 1793 essay *On the common saying: That may be correct in theory, but it does not work in practice*, Kant argues that in theoretical matters, the saying is merely ignorant and foolish, but in morality it provides a cover for moral corruption, by offering specious grounds for making exceptions to valid moral principles (TP 8:276–278). Two years later in the Appendix to *Perpetual Peace*, he offers the two philosophical principles of publicity *not* in order to give politicians and statesmen intellectual counsel on how to reconcile right with politics, but instead solely to warn them against the temptation to corruption when they place political expediency ahead of right (TPP 8:381–386).

Perhaps the most striking thing is that in Kant's view, common rational moral cognition gives *every moral agent roughly equal access* to the truth about what to do. If the men in the cartoon are a university ethics committee, some of them may have PhDs from Ivy League universities, even distinguished named chairs in ethics and a *curriculum vitae* full of publications in peer-reviewed journals and elite university presses. But when it comes to having a moral compass, Kant thinks that Miss Dugan, or the custodian or cleaning lady who lack even a high school education, would be at least as well qualified as they are to *distinguish right from wrong*. "Thus I need no well-informed shrewdness to know what I have to do in order to make my volition morally good" (G 4:403). We need to pause a moment and let this sink in; it might change our view of Kant's ethics:

> Here one cannot regard without admiration the way the practical faculty of judgment is so far ahead of the theoretical in the common

human understanding, [which] can [determine the worth of actions] with just as much hope of getting things right as any philosopher might promise to do; indeed, it is almost more secure in this than the latter, because the philosopher has no other principle than the common understanding, but the philosopher's judgment is easily confused by a multiplicity of considerations that are alien and do not belong to the matter and can make it deviate from the straight direction. (G 4:404)

Kant thinks ordinary people are at least as morally trustworthy as philosophers, even at least as wise.[3] But he is by no means of the opinion that common rational moral cognition is intellectually infallible. He recognizes that even the most conscientious moral agents can commit errors of the understanding on moral questions. These errors may be innocent. That is why he thinks we must engage in conscientious reflection on our decisions and actions, and must follow the verdict of our conscience. Conscience is an inner tribunal in which I am accused, prosecutor, and judge all at once. The issue before the court is not whether what I have done, or am going to do, is objectively right. It is rather whether I have truly done my best to discover what is right, and also to fathom my own true intentions in doing what I do. All that can be asked of us, Kant holds, is that we pronounce a valid verdict of conscience and follow it, even if our action is objectively wrong and based on errors of the understanding. We may be acquitted before the inner court of conscience even if we are in moral error, just as we may be pronounced guilty before this court even in doing the objectively right thing, but not conscientiously (MM 6: 401, 437–440, Rel 6:185–190).

---

[3] On this point, he follows Rousseau. "I am myself by inclination an investigator. I feel a complete thirst for knowledge and an eager unrest to go further in it as well as satisfaction at every acquisition. There was a time when I believed that this alone could constitute the honor of mankind, and I had contempt for the ignorant rabble who know nothing. *Rousseau* brought me around. This blinding superiority disappeared. I learned to honor human beings, and I would find myself far more useless than the common laborer if I did not believe that this consideration could impart to all others a value establishing the rights of humanity" (Ca *Notes and Fragments*, p. 7).

Where Kant most disagrees with many philosophers, both in his own time and today, is on the question what *moral philosophy*, and a moral *principle*, are *for*. He thinks moral agents don't need philosophy to tell them *what to do*. It can offer moral agents only a *canon of judgment*, helping them to find their moral compass, so that they don't – misled by inclinations and self-preference – self-deceptively misapply common rational moral cognition in a particular case. That is the *only* sort of principle Kant is seeking in the First Section of the *Groundwork*.

There is of course a more complete formulation of the moral principle in the *philosophical* account presented in the Second Section of the *Groundwork*. No more than the first formula is this a discursive procedure for making or justifying decisions. Instead it provides philosophical justification for, and a taxonomy of, various *duties* we recognize in everyday life. It also gives us a statement of the supreme principle of morality that aspires (always imperfectly) to be a *doctrine of wisdom* (CPrR 5:108, 130–131, MM 6:375 n, Anth 7:200). True wisdom, however, belongs in Kant's view as much to the untutored common understanding as to the philosopher. Moral philosophy can never do more than ground the duties that common rational moral cognition already recognizes, and explicate in more abstract terms the values and principles it presupposes.

Most of us philosophers still do not agree. We think moral problems do often pose difficult intellectual challenges. Talented and trained minds are more likely to solve them than ordinary and uneducated ones. We need all the help and advice we can get from the Frances Kamms and Jeff McMahans of this world, even if their methods and judgments are far from infallible. So we worry that under the influence of that moralistic social misfit Rousseau, Kant may well be overlooking the element of truth in Wolffian intellectualism. At the same time, Kant and Rousseau might also be right: the mentality of corporate executives and university ethics committees is often just as squalid as Dana Fradon's cartoon is insinuating. We are in bad shape *both* intellectually *and* morally. My point is that if we are to understand Kant's moral philosophy correctly, then we must bracket our own assumptions and read

Kant in terms of his. That's what both Kant's critics and his defenders have too often failed to do.

§4. FUL/FLN: Universalizability as a Canon of Judgment

The priority of FUL/FLN. In the reception of Kant's ethics, FUL and FLN (usually not clearly distinguished from each other) have loomed very large. There are both good and bad reasons for this. The bad reasons I have just been discussing. But there are also some *good* reasons. One is simply that FUL is the *first* formula of the moral law that Kant offers. It is also the formula that philosophically explicates what he thinks ordinary moral agents need a moral principle *for* in everyday life. Other reasons are provided by some of the bold claims Kant makes about FUL/FLN. Kant asserts, to begin with, that there is *only one categorical imperative,* and FUL is it (G 4:421). Then after stating FUL, Kant begins the next sentence: "Now if from this one imperative all imperatives of duty can be derived as from their principle ..." The context suggests that this antecedent is something he wants to assert. Further, after presenting FLN, and then the four famous examples he uses to illustrate its use, Kant says: "Now these are some of the many actual duties, or at least of what we take to be duties, whose derivation from the single principle just adduced clearly meets the eye" (G 4:423–424).[4] But these claims, if

---

[4] There is in fact a serious textual problem with this last sentence. The word I have here translated "derivation" would be correctly so translated if it had been *Ableitung.* But in fact, in both the 1785 and 1786 editions of the *Groundwork,* the word is actually *Abteilung* ("partitioning" or "compartmentalizing"). Beginning with Gustav Hartenstein in 1838, some editors have replaced *Abteilung* with *Ableitung,* supposing that Kant is here only repeating the claim two pages earlier that all duties can be derived (*abgeleitet*) from FUL. Most English translators, including H. J. Paton, Lewis White Beck, Brendan Liddell, James Ellington, Mary Gregor, and Jonathan Bennett, have followed Hartenstein, and for the sake of the present discussion, I am conceding that doubtful emendation. But in the rest of the paragraph Kant argues that maxims violating perfect duties cannot even be thought as universal laws of nature, while maxims violating imperfect duties can be thought but not willed as universal laws of nature. So he does seem more interested in the *classification* of duties than in their *derivation.* Yet if this were his meaning, the word

not read with caution, are sure to mislead us, especially if we combine them with prejudices Kant does not share about what a moral principle is *for* and what it means to *derive* something from one.

On a moment's reflection, we can see that the claims just quoted are hard to make sense of. If FUL is the *only* categorical imperative, then why does Kant go on immediately to formulate *another* categorical imperative (FLN), and then within ten or fifteen pages, three more of them (FH, FA, FRE)? One way of making sense of this claim is suggested by the fact that he already intends to offer more than one formula – in fact a *system* of formulas, "only so many formulas of the very same law" (*nur so viele Formeln eben desselben Gesetzes*) (G 4:436). Kant may at this point already be thinking about his overall plan. He may be making claims about FUL that he intends to be true not of it alone but of the entire system of formulas. Thus when he says there is only one categorical imperative, and *this* is it – referring to his *first* formulation of it – that might be his way not of privileging FUL, but on the contrary of saying that the sole categorical imperative is *this* "very same" law – the one that is about to be stated in a variety of different formulations.

The claims involving the *derivation* of duties are hard to make sense of if they refer to the general positive duties involved in his examples. FUL and FLN propose tests to be applied to particular maxims, one by one, to determine whether they are permissible. If we wanted to use these tests to show, for example, that there is

---

Einteilung (division or classification) rather than *Abteilung* would be more natural. However, in the very opening sentence of the *Groundwork*, Kant did use the verb *sich abteilen* in a way he clearly equated with *Einteilung* (G 4:387). In the recent edition of the *Grundlegung*, Dieter Schönecker and Bernd Kraft follow strictly the Academy Edition and the early editions, reading *Abteilung*. I have agreed with them in my own translation of the *Groundwork*, translating the word as "partitioning." In his revision of Gregor's translation (2012), Jens Timmermann also questions the Hartenstein emendation. Thomas Kingsmill Abbott (in his 1883 translation), also holds fast to the anomalous word *Abteilung*, reading it as if it had been *Einteilung*. For the final clause quoted here, he proposes: "... which obviously fall into the two classes on the one principle we have laid down."

a general duty not to commit suicide, or to keep the promises we make, we would have to consider each and every maxim on which one might conceivably propose to kill oneself or make a promise without keeping it, and then somehow demonstrate that *none* of these possible maxims can be willed to be a universal law (or law of nature). But this seems impossible, or at least to involve a complex project of grouping maxims together and showing that all of certain classes fail the universalizability test. More to the point, Kant never tries to do any such thing. Kant never actually claims *to derive any* general duties from either FUL or FLN; he says at most that *we can see that they are derived.* Since we are never given an actual derivation of any duty from these formulas, we don't really know what he means by a 'derivation.' Nor do we even know precisely *what* is being derived: Is it the general duty not to commit suicide? Or is it only this one *application* by judgment of this duty to this agent's proposed action and maxim? Cautious attention to what he actually does would suggest we read it the latter way. Those arguments, however, do not even explicitly *state* the general duties involved in the examples. In fact, if we look carefully at Kant's handling of the four examples, we see that in relation to FLN, he introduces the four duties not by deriving them but only by "enumerating" (*herzählen*) them (G 4:421). The enumeration is divided according to a taxonomy he explicitly describes as "discretionary" and whose justification he leaves to a "future metaphysics of morals" (G 4:421 n).

Perhaps Kant's suggestion that imperatives of duty are derived from FUL does not mean that all duties can be derived from *that* specific formula, but instead that they are derived from *some* formula of the one "very same" moral law of which, again, this is the first formula to be presented. For clearly they cannot all be derived from FUL *alone* and then *also* be seen to be derived from the different formula FLN, as Kant says only two pages later (accepting the dubious textual emendation discussed in note 4). If we are attentive, we can even identify *which* later formula it is from which Kant does explicitly derive (*ableiten*) the four general duties. In considering the four examples in relation to FH, an explicit statement of each duty is provided, and FH is also said to be "a supreme practical ground . . .

from which all laws of the will must be able to be derived (*abgeleitet*)" (G 4:429–430). (We will return to this point later, in our discussion of FH.) It is a common criticism of FUL/FLN that these formulas *presuppose* determinate duties rather than *supplying* or *deriving* them (for instance see Hegel, 1991, §135 R, A). Such critics seem oblivious to the fact that Kant's actual use of FUL/FLN in the *Groundwork* fully *accepts* this point and even *depends on* it.

There is yet one more *good* reason why FUL/FLN has been regarded as having priority in relation to the other formulas. Both in the First Section, where Kant developed it out of the thought that moral worth attaches only to actions done from duty, and in the Second Section, where he bases it on the formal aspect of the concept of a categorical imperative, FUL proclaims universal legislation, even universal legislation relating to what every rational being can will, as a moral standard. In that sense, FUL could even be called the *basic* formula of the categorical imperative. The thought that the moral law is a universal law that can be regarded as arising from the volition of every rational being is going to be the central claim of Kant's entire ethical theory, as it will eventually appear in its full form in FA/FRE. We will see presently that the standard of judgment, the impermissibility tests for maxims, set up by FUL and by FLN, are quite distinct tests. And both are also distinct from, and notably weaker than, the standard of "legislative form" operative in FA. (We will return to this point later in discussing FA.) But it is understandable, and a plausible conjecture about Kant's intentions, that his readers are meant to be impressed by his first declaration of the crucial thought that maxims should be thought and willed to be universal laws. Notice, however, that the priority this gives to FUL/FLN is really a priority shared with, or even properly speaking owed to, the later formula FA/FRE, which also turns out to be the only *complete* formula of the supreme principle of morality.

FUL/FLN as general tests of permissibility or as canons of judgment. It has been common in the reception of Kant's ethics to take FUL/FLN to be general tests of permissibility, supposedly capable of giving the "right" result when applied to any and every "maxim" that could be brought before them for testing. The moral agent proposes a maxim (either out of the blue, so to speak, or else based on inclination or prudence) and then tests it for universalizability. That test is precisely what the famous four-step CI-Procedure consists in. This would fit one way that many moral philosophers have thought morality relates to our lives. They suppose the main business of our lives consists in our loves, causes, projects, and self-interest that give our lives happiness and meaning. These would be the source of our "maxims." Morality is then a set of side-constraints brought to bear on our real and authentic lives, telling us No when we go too far toward being our real selves. This invites the objections philosophers such as Bernard Williams (1981), Susan Wolf (2003), and Samuel Scheffler (1992), raise against morality when they worry about the way the inhuman demandingness of its excessive impartiality threatens our individuality and integrity.

One response to these worries, which has been offered by Scheffler, and also by Herman (1993), is to argue that morality does not demand too much of us and allows us to be ourselves after all. Whatever the merits of such replies, the trouble with the whole controversy is that it totally misrepresents the moral life as Kant sees it. Kant sees our lives as rationally self-governed, first and foremost, precisely because in substance our life is devoted to our *moral vocation*. Our basic ends are themselves to be drawn from our duties – mostly our imperfect duties. These ends *include* our loves, our friendships, our projects, our commitments to others, the causes we champion in our lives. There is also a place permitted for our own happiness, but our lives have meaning mostly through ends and maxims that fall under moral duty and do not come from outside it. As we will see presently, our moral duties involve *partiality* of many kinds.[5] It follows that the moral law is *never* to be seen

---

[5] This is true of German idealist ethics more generally. For Fichte and Hegel too the ethical standpoint is our own authentic individual standpoint, not something external to it which limits or constrains it. Neither in Kant, nor Fichte, nor Hegel is the ethical standpoint impartial in the way it is in utilitarianism. The birthplace of these problems is Bentham's paradoxical combination of psychological egoism with a moral standard that seeks the general happiness of society, or of all humanity, or even all sentient creation; its hereditary disease

merely as a permissibility test that says No to us when we press our own authentic desires and projects too far. Morality for Kant is shot through with the *admirable* kinds of partiality that Williams and Wolf think must be *saved from* morality in the name of individual integrity. This is important to emphasize, because the formulas FUL/FLN do involve the standpoint of impartial or universal reason brought to bear on judgment. But if we let these formulas take over Kantian ethics, we force it into the same mold as other theories that are rooted in a different kind of impartiality.[6]

Immediately after presenting the four examples, Kant tells us what they have all been about:

> Now if we attend to ourselves in every transgression of a duty, then we find that we do not actually will that our maxim should become a universal law, for that is impossible for us, but rather will that its opposite should remain a law generally; yet we take the liberty of making an *exception* for ourselves, or (even only for this once) for the advantage of our inclination. Consequently, if we weighed everything from one and the same point of view, namely that of reason, then we would encounter a contradiction in our own will, namely that objectively a certain principle should be necessary as a universal law and yet subjectively that it should not be universally valid, but rather that it should admit of exceptions. But since we consider our action at one time from a point of view that accords entirely with reason, and then, however, also the same action from the point of view of a will affected by inclination, there is actually no contradiction here, but only a resistance of inclination against the precept of reason (*antagonismus*), through which the universality of the principle (*universalitas*) is

---

is Sidgwick's troubled "dualism of practical reason." But German idealist ethics never had these problems to begin with. See Wood (1991, pp. 170–172, 196–206, 238–242) and Wood (2016, pp. 220–244). But CI-Proceduralist readings of Kant would saddle Kantian ethics with them.

[6] Most (neo-) Kantians are sensitive to this mismatch, and try to correct for it. For instance, Christine Korsgaard holds that the maxims we begin with are already expressions of our self-constituted identity as rational, autonomous agents (see Korsgaard, 1996b, 2009). But the corrective medicine comes too late to cure the basic sickness. For this self-constituted identity still has its origin entirely outside morality (perhaps even in our brute animality).

transformed into a mere general validity (*generalitas*), so that the practical principle of reason is supposed to meet the maxim halfway. Now although this cannot be justified in our own impartially rendered judgment, it proves that we actually recognize the validity of the categorical imperative and (with every respect for it) allow ourselves only a few exceptions, which are, as it seems to us, insignificant and forced upon us. (G 4:424)

In none of the four examples is the real starting point simply a "maxim" proposed by the agent. The starting point is always *moral tension* between a determinate *duty* and a possible *action* (or omission) to which an agent is tempted. The maxim expresses this tension, presenting the agent's problem of moral judgment, for which FLN is to serve as a standard or "canon." It offers a defense of the exception to the duty to which we are tempted, but also seeks a fair hearing for the duty. If we place ourselves in the shoes of the agent in each example, then we can see clearly that the maxim in each case is formulated precisely with the aim of explicating the tension in theoretical terms. It is designed to express the agent's temptation and at the same time the agent's intention to give the issue of moral judgment a fair hearing. The maxim articulates the agent's reasons for being tempted – the *real reasons*, not some bogus rationalization that might better justify an action (for a different action, a different agent, or in a different case). It presents these reasons in a way that gives the proposed action the best moral defense the agent might honestly manage, based on the actual temptation. The maxim is supposed to articulate both sides of the case, so that the judgment is fair.[7]

---

[7] I submit that the standard so-called "puzzle maxims" (Timmermann, 2007, pp. 77–78) or alleged "false-positives" and "false-negatives" (Wood, 1999, pp. 102–107) that have been used to challenge FUL/FLN could never even come up for testing at all if these formulas were used in the way Kant intends. The "false-negatives" are maxims that plainly conform to duty, so they could not represent the moral tension for which the formulas are designed. The "false-positives" are maxims that include morally irrelevant details and are obviously designed to elude the universalizability test. This last point has often been made by Kantians in response to such maxims, but that reply would be utterly irrelevant if FUL/FLN were intended simply to be general permissibility tests for maxims regarded as general policies of action. If what we are trying to determine is the

The man tempted to suicide, for instance, feels sorry for himself due to a "series of ills that have accumulated to the point of hope-lessness." His maxim is designed to offer this attitude as a *defense* for his contemplated act of suicide (G 4:421–422). Likewise, in the second example, the maxim offers *Geldnot* – financial distress or emergency – as a possible justification for the making of a promise he does not intend to keep (G 4:422). Here the term *Not* is an attempt to invoke a "right of necessity" (or emergency) – a defense someone might offer for doing something that would normally be wrong, but can, in unusual or extreme circumstances, be either justified or at least excused (G 4:422; cf. 4:402, cf. MM 6:235–236). Similar moves are evident in the other two examples, as we will see later. These maxims are *never* meant to formulate general policies of action to be tested for their general permissibility. They are designed to put the issue of right and wrong for *this* decision fairly before the agent's own faculty of moral judgment, taking into account the universal standpoint of reason. The question is *never*: "Can I, or can anyone, permissibly act on this maxim?" but rather *always*: "Does this

general permissibility of a policy (e.g. "Help the poor," "Refuse all bribes," "Give more to charity than the average person does," "Buy clockwork trains but never sell them," "Make a false promise on a Tuesday to a person named Hildreth Milton Flitcraft") then it is obviously irrelevant to the issue whether it is the "real maxim" on which any particular agent is acting. The only relevant question would be whether the tests get the "wrong" result. If they were supposed to be part of a general CI-Procedure, these maxims (or at least some of them) would show the tests and the procedure, to be unreliable. We could then argue that they can't be trusted even in cases where they might happen to get the right results. I suggest that those who reply to these counterexamples by saying: "this isn't the agent's *real* maxim" are at least implicitly aware of the restrictions I have just been describing on Kant's use of FUL/FLN. But then they are trying inconsistently to combine this awareness with the persisting pretense that FUL/FLN can after all be used as general tests for the permissibility of maxims after the manner of a "CI-Procedure." They still cling to the basically un-Kantian idea of what a moral principle is *for*. Even more artificial replies to these examples are offered by those who quibble over what counts as a "maxim" and claim that the alleged counter-examples aren't "maxims" at all. This is especially unconvincing when they have to admit they can't even tell you how to distinguish something that's "really a maxim" from something that's not one (see Allison, 2011, pp. 198–199). For further discussion of this point, see Wood (2017b, §§ 3–4).

maxim offer me, under *these* circumstances, a sufficient justification for exempting myself from *this* duty?"

The questions posed by the universalizability tests are therefore the following:

1. Does this maxim offer a reason – a morally acceptable justification or excuse – for this action or omission such that, in relation to this particular duty, I could will that any agent might use this reason in circumstances like mine to exempt themselves from this specific duty?
2. If, with the regularity of a law of nature, all rational beings, under my circumstances, were to use this maxim as their justification or excuse for exempting themselves from this duty, could I will to be a member of such an order of things?

§5. *The Universalizability Tests: Their Mechanics*

There is a noteworthy difference between these two questions. The first is the question put by FUL, and the second is the one put by FLN. FUL asks whether you can will your maxim to be a universal *law* – that is, a universal *norm*. FLN, by contrast, asks whether I can will that my maxim be a *universal law of nature* – that is, can I will that it *actually be followed* by people in my situation with the regularity of a universal law of nature, when also combined with other laws and facts of nature (including human nature) as we know them?[8]

First stage: "Suppose your maxim were a universal law (or law of nature). What then?" Kant's arguments depend on certain premises that are designed to help answer those questions:

FUL: Premises about norms. In relation to the question posed by FUL, Kant asks: "When in a tight spot, may I [*darf ich*] not make

---

[8] Kant seems to think that the second question is more "intuitive" or closer to "feeling." But it is the first question he imagines the agent posing in the First Section, so maybe he thinks the less intuitive and more austere question is the one most suitable to aid the ordinary person's moral *judgment*. I won't try to sort this out here. We will face a related puzzle at the very end of this essay, concerning what Kant calls the "universal formula" (G 4:436–437).

a promise with the intention of not keeping it? ... Would I be able to say to myself that anyone may [*mag jedermann*] make an untruthful promise when he finds himself in embarrassment that he cannot get out of in any other way?" (G 4:402–403). The argument is that then there would properly be no promises at all, and also "it would be pointless to avow my will in regard to future actions to those who would not believe the avowal, or if they rashly did so, who would pay me back in the same coin" (G 4:403). If the maxim were a universal norm, then it would be pointless to avow one's future intentions, at least with the aim of getting some consideration in return (e.g. the money one wants to borrow) because no one would lend you money in return for an avowal that does not obligate. Kant also observes that if I rashly gave something to others in exchange for such an avowal, they would then be permitted not to do what I was counting on them to do ("pay me back in the same coin").

FLN: Premises about natural laws. In response to the question posed by FLN, the argument is different. Kant claims that such a law of nature, inserted into a world otherwise the same as ours, "would make impossible the promise and the end one might have in making it, since no one would believe what was promised him but rather would laugh at every such utterance as vain pretense" (G 4:422). Both arguments claim that under the conditions supposed, the *promise itself* would be impossible – but for quite different reasons. A *norm* that would permit people to make promises they don't intend to keep would contradict the very concept of a promise; that's why it would make promises impossible. Willing that there be a *law of nature* that people make untruthful promises when it got them out of an emergency would make your promise itself impossible because in a nature otherwise like the present one, people could anticipate that under these circumstances others would never do what they promise, and therefore nothing you said could *function* as a promise – i.e. it could not obtain for you the credit you seek. It is not yet clear why in either case this would make it impossible for the agent to will the maxim to be a universal law (or law of nature). We will return to those questions presently. The argument from FLN adds that in a world in which people knew that promises (or pretended promises) like mine would not be kept, they would only laugh at me, so that I could not achieve the end I sought in making the false promise. That is a further consequence of your maxim's being a universal law (or law of nature) to which Kant will appeal in arguing that you cannot will such a thing.

Must the premises in Kant's arguments be "purely factual"? It is sometimes claimed that the premises used in these arguments other than FUL and FLN themselves must be purely factual premises having no moral content. O'Neill has particularly insisted on this point (O'Neill, 2013 [1975], Chapters 2 and 3). I have never understood why the premises used in these arguments would have to be only "factual." I fear this constraint arises from a model of moral reasoning I have said Kant is *not* using in these arguments: namely, the idea that a moral principle constitutes a *normative* principle which, when combined with purely *factual* information, is supposed to provide us with a discursive procedure for deciding what to do or a criterion distinguishing right actions from wrong ones. Of course in using FLN, Kant's claims about laws of nature, and about what nature would be like if the agent's maxim were added to them as another law of nature, are meant to be factual claims about nature and its laws. But the claim used in FUL, that I could not will the maxim to be a universal norm, looks like a *normative* claim, not a factual one. Moreover, once we see how the universalizability tests work, we see that even the "factual" claims used in FLN involve *normative* principles (even if not *morally* normative principles) about what an agent *can and cannot rationally will* – on instrumental or prudential grounds. If we look at the task of FUL/FLN as providing a canon of judgment, there seems to be no good reason at all why we could not be guided in the correct application of concepts like good, evil, and duty to particular cases by normative thoughts as well as by purely factual thoughts.

Second stage: "*Can you will* your maxim to be a universal law (universal law of nature)?" In order to get from Kant's premises about what would follow if your maxim were a universal law (or law of nature) to his conclusions – that you could not *will* it to be one – we need the answers to three questions:

First: Who are "you"? Who is supposed to answer the question whether *you* can will the maxim to be a universal law (or a law of nature)? In other words, which properties of the agent who asks this question are we taking into account, and from which properties are we abstracting?

Second: What does it mean to "be able to will"? What sort of conative act or attitude is "willing"? What does it mean to *be able* to will something, as distinct from *actually* willing it?

Third: How do you decide whether you can will your maxim to be a universal law? That is, based on the answer to the second question, what are the *standards, norms,* or *criteria* for "being able to will"? Let's take these three questions one by one and try to answer them.

First: *You* are simply a finite rational being under the general conditions of human life. The point of these universalizability .ests, as Kant tells us a page later, is to help the agent "weigh everything from one and the same point of view, namely that of reason" (G 4:424). Therefore, I think the most plausible answer to the first question is that "you" are yourself – but considered only as a rational human being, abstracting as far as possible from features of yourself that might get in the way of your weighing things from a universal and rational human point of view. After all, the problem FUL and FLN are meant to address is that the agent's judgment is likely to be distorted by looking at things in a way that exaggerates the value and importance of that agent's inclinations and self-love. It is for these distortions of judgment that the first formula of the moral law is meant to correct. This may also help us with the answer to the third question, since we may suppose that the criteria for what we can and can't will are also intended to be only those available from the universal standpoint of reason.

Second: *Willing* is choosing. For Kant (as for Aristotle, NE 1111b12–32), *will* (or *choice*) is a species of desire distinct from *wish*. We may wish for things without being able to do anything about it, or even wish for the impossible, but we can will (or choose) only those objects we can set as ends and then take some means toward making them actual (G 4:394, MM 6:213,

452, Anth 7:251). Being *able to will* is therefore *being able to choose*. This means I can will only what I suppose to be possible. I may wish, will, and even choose, to eat my cake, and then *wish* I had the same piece of cake still to eat even after I have eaten it. But after eating the cake, I cannot *will* still to have it.

Thus *being able* to will that your maxim is a universal law or law of nature is being able to choose to bring it about, supposing hypothetically (and counterfactually) that you were in a position to make such a choice, that it is a universal law or law of nature. Of course none of us are ever in that position, since our wills cannot arbitrarily establish moral norms or prescribe laws to nature. But there are nevertheless certain minimal criteria that some imagined state of affairs would have to satisfy in order for us to *be able* to will or choose something, supposing it were it in our power to choose it. Namely: in order to be able to will something, that thing must *first*, be possible in itself, and *second*, our volition must not conflict with other choice we must have made if we are rational. These general considerations provide the sole rational criteria used in Kant's arguments from FLN.

Third: The two tests for universalizability: Being able to *think* and being able to *will*. In Kant's discussion of the four examples in relation to FLN, he draws a distinction between being able to *think* your maxim as a universal law of nature and being able to *will* that it should be one.[9] Part of his reasoning seems to be that if a maxim cannot even be thought to be a universal law of nature, then it cannot be willed to be one, since we might *wish for*, but cannot *choose*, what we cannot think possible. In the literature, especially the "CI-Procedure" literature, there is a set of accepted terms for the kinds of reasons that make it impossible for us to will maxims to be universal laws.[10] The "contradiction in conception" test is

---

[9] Kant also appears to think that this difference tells us something about these two kinds of duties, or enables us to classify them, as the original word *Abteilung* at G 4:424 might perhaps imply (again, see Note 4). I doubt that he is right about this, but I won't look into that issue here. I have discussed it in Wood (1999, pp. 97–102). See also Herman (1993, Chapter 6).

[10] For a few prominent discussions of these matters, see O'Neill (2013 [1975]); O'Neill (1989, Chapter 5); Herman (1993, Chapters 6 and 7); Korsgaard (1996a,

distinguished from the "contradiction in the will" test, and two different versions of the former test are distinguished: "logical interpretation" and the "practical interpretation." I accept the standard taxonomy of these reasons, and will now even attempt to provide my own brief rationale for it.

Contradiction in conception. If you are to be able to will something, that thing must at least be possible – not self-contradictory. It must also be consistent with whatever else you are thinking of as conditions of its possibility. In relation to FUL, being able to will your maxim to be a universal law (or norm) would require that it be consistent with other norms you recognize. In relation to the false promising example, the obvious norm is that in the circumstances you are thinking about, promises create obligations. Thus to will the false promising maxim to be a universal law, you would have to will it to be a universal norm that people in your situation would make promises that obligate but which they are permitted not to keep – in other words, that do not obligate. So you can't will that.

In relation to FLN, this first condition has *two* consequences, which provide two *different* ways in which it might be impossible even to *think* your maxim to be at the same time a universal law of nature:

The logical interpretation. We cannot choose, even under imagined hypothetical circumstances, things we know to be impossible. Therefore we cannot will them. In relation to the false promising example, this makes it clear why it is not jointly possible to will my maxim and also to will it to be a universal law of nature. If my maxim were a universal law of nature, promises made under my circumstances would never be kept, and in nature as we know it to be, people would come to know this. My intended promise could not then function as promise – as Kant says, the *promise itself* would be impossible. I cannot will both to act on my maxim, making this promise, and at the same time (*zugleich*) that my

Chapter 3); Wood (1999, Chapter 3); Rawls (2000, pp. 170–175); Allison (2011, Chapter 7); Guyer (2014 [2006], Chapter 5). But some of the claims involved in the use of these terms are still sometimes disputed (for instance, see Rivera-Castro, 2014, and Kleingeld, 2017).

maxim should be a universal law of nature, since then promises would be impossible. The reason for the *zugleich* should be obvious: I am considering a possible excuse for *an action I intend to perform* if the excuse is acceptable. FLN tests the excuse from the standpoint of reason by asking whether I could *also* (along with doing as I intend, hence *at the same time*) will the maxim to be a universal law of nature.

The practical interpretation. As we've just seen, it is part of the FUL test that you should not only be able to will your maxim to be a universal law of nature, but also that you should be able to do this at the same time (*zugleich*) that you will the maxim itself – as in: choosing the particular action whose dutifulness you are trying to determine through judgment. So what I must be able to will is *both* that I successfully perform the action and also, *at the same time*, that my maxim should be a universal law of nature. But it is also the case that to set an end is to will that it become actual through the means I take to it if other circumstances make this possible. I cannot self-consistently choose to set an end and take certain means toward it and *also* choose that these means should necessarily fail to achieve the end. If I were to will my false promising maxim to be a universal law of nature, then given the other facts of nature as I know them, I would have to will *also* that my promise not be believed, so that the person would not lend me the money I need. In other words, as Kant also says, I'd need to will that *the end to be achieved by my promise* would not be possible. Therefore, I could not self-consistently will both my maxim, which includes the end involved in it, and also that my maxim become a universal law of nature, since that would require me to will that the means I take toward the end should necessarily fail.

It might be questioned whether the practical interpretation is really a case of a *contradiction in conception*; it seems to involve a *contradiction in the will* – between your *willing* your present action and your also *willing* that its maxim be a universal law of nature. But there is still a crucial difference that makes the practical interpretation a kind of contradiction in conception and distinguishes it from a contradiction in the will. A contradiction in the will involves a conflict between willing your maxim to be a universal law of nature and also willing *something else* (something falling outside the maxim) which, as a rational human being, you necessarily do will. But in the case of the practical interpretation, the conflict of volitions is internal to willing your own maxim and *at the same time* willing that same maxim to be a universal law of nature. So it is a contradiction in the very conception of a nature in which (1) you act as you propose to act and at the same time (2) your maxim is a universal law of that nature. It is a contradiction internal to the conception of a nature in which these two things simultaneously hold.

The distinction between the logical and practical interpretations is often presented as a contest between two rival *versions* of the contradiction in conception. I have never been able to understand why they are supposed to be rivals. They are both explicitly present in Kant's own text regarding the false promising example: If the false promising maxim were a universal law of nature, then the *promise itself* would be impossible (the logical interpretation), and also *the end to be achieved by it* would be impossible (the practical interpretation). Both arguments are also sound. Each, independently of the other, shows it to be impossible to will the maxim and simultaneously that it be a universal law of nature.

Contradiction in the will. Again, the test involved in FUL/FLN is not only whether you could will your maxim to be a universal law (or universal law of nature) but also whether you could *at the same time act* on your maxim – that is, actually perform the proposed action, using this maxim as an excuse or justification for exempting yourself from the duty you suspect it might violate. In order to be able to choose something, I must not also actually choose, or be required rationally to choose, something else that is incompatible with it. So if there are some things which every rational human being necessarily wills, then no human being can will any other thing that is incompatible with that. Thus if willing my maxim to be a universal law of nature conflicts with something else I necessarily will as a rational human being, then I cannot will my maxim to be a universal law of nature. We will see presently that this is essential to both of the last two examples – of the imperfect duties to develop some of one's talents and to show sympathy and beneficence toward someone you see to be in need.

§6. *The Four Examples*

First example: Suicide. Kant obviously chose his four examples because he thought the duties they involve would be readily accepted by common rational moral cognition. This may have been true in relation to his time and culture, but some of Kant's conclusions, especially the one about suicide, might themselves be questioned on substantive moral grounds. Is there a general moral duty – even a duty to oneself – not to commit suicide? It is worth stressing that Kant's example assumes there is such a duty, and the question is only whether the agent's maxim could justify making an exception to it. Many of us would now sooner side with the position of Hume – shockingly controversial in the eighteenth century but much less so now – that there is no such general duty.[11] Thus not only the conclusion of his argument, but even the unquestioned assumption of a general duty, and also the main premise in Kant's argument from FLN might well be doubted. (I myself doubt all three.) But these doubts do not affect the validity of FLN itself as illustrated in the example, so long as we see that if we grant the assumed (questionable) duty, and the (dubious) premise, then the (dubious) conclusion follows. Which it clearly does.

---

[11] Hume (2005 [1783]). Hume suppressed the essay on suicide based (as he said) on "prudence" and also perhaps on his friend Adam Smith's advice (see Mossner, 1970, pp. 322–323). Kant's own views on this topic are much more complex and ambivalent than people realize if they have read only the *Groundwork*. Kant himself was clearly troubled by the fact that sometimes suicide serves as a way of defending one's human dignity, as was portrayed in Joseph Addison's well-known play about Cato's suicide (see L-Eth-Collins 27: 370–375). In the Casuistical Questions, Kant offers a half-dozen arguments, without giving any clear replies to them, in favor of various acts that might be regarded as suicide (MM 6:423–424). I think we should infer that whatever Kant's own considered views about suicide might have been, he could imagine intelligent readers siding with one or more of these arguments.

Kant's argument depends on a premise about the natural purpose or vocation (*Bestimmung*) of self-love in the human being: that this is "the furtherance of life." The claim is then that when the agent appeals to his impulse of self-love as the reason for his suicide – using this, by means of his maxim, as the justification for the act – the maxim in question cannot be made consistent with a system of nature in which it is supposed at the same time to be a universal law of nature. It could not be viewed as an acceptable ground for making an exception to the assumed duty to preserve one's life. I think we can agree that if the natural purpose of human self-love were to promote the survival of the individual human organism, then this would involve a contradiction in conception in the thought of a nature one of whose universal laws was that self-love would systematically lead to the self-destruction of the organism. The inference is clearly valid according to the pattern of reasoning we have drawn from FLN.

At a deeper level, Kant's argument here seems to be appealing to a traditional principle in the natural law tradition: that we ought to respect the natural purposiveness involved in our nature and not act against it by using parts of our nature contrary to their natural ends. Kant uses a similar mode of argument in arguing that there is an ethical duty to oneself not to lie, since lying violates the natural purposiveness of speech (MM 6:429). He also seriously considers a parallel argument that if reproduction is the natural purpose of sex, then it would be "self-defilement" to engage in sexual intercourse under conditions where pregnancy could not result. In this Casuistical Question Kant appears to resist this (ghastly) conclusion – as involving "purism (a pedantry regarding the fulfillment of duty, as far as the wideness of the obligation is concerned)" (MM 6:426). Arguments of this form, if they are to be convincing, depend on quite specific judgments about natural purposiveness as well as about what conduct does and does not respect it. Such arguments require good judgment on both counts, making them easy targets for parody.[12]

---

[12] The Marquis de Sade cites the natural purposiveness of both self-love and the human impulses with which his own name has become synonymous, arguing (disingenuously) that we have a natural duty to be both selfish and cruel (Sade, 1966 [1791], pp. 253–255, 349–367). For Kant some features of our natural

We might consider Kant's argument more sympathetically if we looked at the agent's maxim through the lens of some of Kant's own sober convictions about the human condition. The agent states his reason for contemplating suicide as follows: "I make it my principle to shorten my life when by longer term it promises more ill than agreeableness" (G 4:422). In his self-pity, he seems to regard his own condition as unusually grim, hence permitting an exception to the assumed general prohibition on suicide. But is the agent's predicament, as represented by the maxim, really so unusual? Kant does not think so. "The value of life for us, if it is assessed in terms of what one enjoys, is easy to decide. It sinks below zero; for who would enter life anew under the same conditions, or even according to a new, self-projected plan (though in conformity with the course of nature) were it set merely toward enjoyment?" (CJ 5:434 n). If it holds generally, perhaps universally, for all human lives, that at every point they promise more ill than agreeableness, then this agent's maxim, if it were followed as a universal law of nature, would result in *everyone's* committing suicide. Perhaps we must agree that a nature in which that was a universal law would involve a contradiction in conception. The maxim no longer looks like a good excuse for exempting himself, *as an exceptional case*, from the *presupposed general duty* not to kill oneself.

Second example: False promising. Kant's example of the false promise has been discussed above when we illustrated how the universalizability tests in FUL and FLN work. I won't repeat what was said there. But certain easily imaginable variants on this example can help us to understand the proper function and limits of the canon of judgment FUL/FLN are meant to provide.

---

teleology clearly go contrary to morality, while some harmonize with it. Sensible appeals to natural teleology must take this into account. Kant holds that human unsociable sociability – competitiveness and self-conceit – serve the natural purpose of inciting the human species to develop its natural predispositions (IUH 8:20–22). But he also holds that we have a duty to unite our ends with those of others, that arrogance is a vice opposed to our duty of respect toward others (MM 6:465–466), and that it is the fundamental vocation of moral feeling to strike down self-conceit (CPrR 5:73).

Legitimate promise-breaking and false promise-making. Since all of Kant's examples are cases where an agent attempts to justify an exception or exemption to a recognized duty, we should see on reflection that their background assumption is that in principle there *could* be justified cases of this kind – cases where a proposed action seems to be prohibited by a certain duty but the action be perfectly innocent or perhaps morally meritorious or even required.

In real life, promises always include tacit and reasonable hedges. Suppose you have borrowed money from me and promised to repay it at a certain time and place, but it turns out that when you are scheduled to do this, an unexpected emergency arises: the only way for you to save someone's life (for instance, the life of your own child) is for you not to show up. Instead you may even have to spend the money you were going to pay me in order to preserve your child's life in this unexpected emergency. This might be a genuine case of *Geldnot*: even I, to whom the money is owed, if I were at all reasonable, would think you should be released (at least temporarily) from the obligation to keep your promise. We could then surely formulate a maxim that articulates your justification, and it would pass the FUL and FLN universalizability tests.

Likewise, we can easily think of cases where you would be justified in *making a promise you don't intend to keep*. Suppose a gang of criminals has kidnapped your child and threatens to kill it unless you promise to make yourself complicit in a murder. You make the promise, but then devise a clever plan where they first release your child and then you break your promise, preventing the crime. Your maxim in this case could be: "I will make a promise without intending to keep it if the promise is made under duress and it is a promise to do something that is in itself wrong." That maxim would surely pass the FUL/FLN universalizability tests. Promises made under duress are usually regarded as invalid, and an action wrong in itself should not be done even if you promised to do it. A nature in which everyone followed your maxim would not render impossible or counter-purposive any promises we consider binding.

Passing the test is no guarantee of permissibility. Would the fact that this maxim passes the FUL/FLN tests show that actions in conformity with it are morally justified? I think we'd agree that your actions in this case are morally justified, but I don't think Kant is committed to saying that this could be demonstrated just by the fact that the maxim passes these tests. Nowhere in Kant's writings (No, not even once!) does he use FUL/FLN to conclude that an action or a maxim is *permissible* because it *passes* a FUL/FLN universalizability test.[13] It is possible, consistent with everything Kant ever says, that there might be actions whose maxims pass the test but those actions are impermissible for some other reason. What this illustrates, I believe, is *first*, that the FUL/FLN tests are only *sine qua non* tests of permissibility, and *second*, that no canon of judgment is necessarily suited to every situation or can be guaranteed to solve every problem of judgment to which someone might apply it. To suppose that FUL/FLN must provide a foolproof guarantee against bad or corrupted judgment would be to demand the impossible of these formulas, and of moral philosophy more generally.

Interlude: Kant on Moral Rules and Kinds of Duties

As we move from a discussion of the perfect to the imperfect duties, it will help if we clarify some things about how Kant thinks of duties and their taxonomy.

Moral rules and exceptions. The examples with which FUL/ FLN deal are matters of judgment –the application to particular cases of general moral concepts: "good, evil, duty, contrary to duty" (G 4:403).[14] More specifically, these are examples in which we

---

[13] For reasons we will explore later in §8, it is *not* an exception to this claim when Kant regards the maxim of prudence: "Pursue your own happiness," as legislative when you include the happiness of others among your ends as well (CPrR 5:34, MM 6:451).

[14] One of Kant's twelve "categories of freedom" (CPrR 5:66) is "practical rules of exception (*exceptivae*)." It appears to be a category combining that of rules of commission with that of rules of omission, just as in the theoretical categories, *limitation* combines *reality* with *negation* (CPR A80/B106). As I understand *exceptivae*, it is a concept covering cases where you would be obligated to do

could describe the agent as wondering whether an *exception* can be made to a moral rule or duty. But there is more than one way of thinking about "making exceptions to moral rules," and Kant's way of thinking about this is different from the way most people probably think about it.

Most people tend to think of moral rules as requiring or prohibiting certain kinds of actions when given a morally neutral description. For instance, "Do not lie" means something like: "Do not intentionally say something that you know to be untrue." Then of course we run across cases in which such acts of speaking falsely look morally justified – e.g. lying (in this sense of the term) to the murderer at the door.[15] The moral rule is therefore regarded as valid only generally, not universally, and that's what we mean when we say it is subject to "exceptions" – cases in which a rule that holds generally does not hold in that particular case. This is how Mill, for instance, thinks about it when he says that "it is not the fault of any creed, but of the complicated nature of human affairs, that rules of conduct cannot be framed so as to admit of no exceptions" (Mill, 2001, p. 25). This is certainly one natural way to think about "rules and exceptions." But it is not the only way, and it is definitely *not* Kant's way. Recall what we saw earlier: Kant regards it as corrupt *ever* to convert the *universalitas* of a duty into a mere *generalitas* (G 4:424). He is thereby declaring that every true duty is *by its concept* universal and *as a matter of principle* admits of no possible exceptions. This might be thought to involve Kant's notorious moral inflexibility or "rigorism." But it involves no such thing, and we need to see why.

A were it not that you have an even stronger obligating reason not to do A – and, as Kant says, *fortior obligandi ratio vincit* (MM 6:224). This might include the case where you would be obligated to pay back the money were it not for the fact that you must take emergency action to save your child, or where you would be obligated not to make the promise to help the criminals kill someone were it not for the fact that they are holding your child hostage and they are making you promise to do something wrong.

[15] For my account of what is really going on in Kant's discussion of Benjamin Constant's example of the murderer at the door, see Wood (2008, Chapter 14).

For Kant, questions about "rules and exceptions" are questions about the correct application by judgment of concepts that designate duties, virtues, or vices. Aristotle too considers some actions by their concept always wrong: Temperance is always good; intemperance and insensibility are always bad; courage is always good, cowardice and rashness are always bad. And so on through the other virtues and vices (NE, 1107a–1109b27). Obviously, the fact that in Kantian ethics all cases of lying, servility, or malice are wrong does not entail that it has unreasonably strict or inflexible moral standards about these matters, any more than the corresponding claims by Aristotle imply unreasonable strictness. For both philosophers, these are matters to be decided by sound moral *judgment* or φρόνησις.

Kantian duties are a system of concepts which designate kinds of actions that are, by the rules of duty, required, forbidden, or meritorious. Suicide, unchastity, self-stupefaction, lying, avarice, and servility are unexceptionably *forbidden* by duty (MM 6: 422–437); so are envy, ingratitude, malice, contempt, arrogance, defamation, ridicule, and the giving and taking of scandal (MM 6: 458–461, 464–468); self-respect and respect for others are strictly *required* by duty (MM 6:435, 462–464); beneficence, gratitude, sympathy, striving for greater virtue and to act from the motive of duty are always *meritorious* (MM 6:452–458, 446–447, 392–393). These claims hold necessarily and without exception simply because duty-concepts are *not* (morally neutral) descriptive concepts: the moral judgments are built into their very meaning.[16] Knowingly to speak falsely, for Kant, is designated by the concept *falsiloquium*; but a lie (*Lüge, mendacium*) is a *falsiloquium dolosum* (a *wrongful* speaking falsely). All *lies* are necessarily wrongful, but not all *falsiloquia* are lies (MM 6:238). Questions of moral judgment do not concern which acts of *lying* are wrong (since all are, by the very concept 'lie'). The question is rather which acts of false speaking count as *lies*.

---

[16] For a discussion of moralized and non-moralized concepts, in which I recommend using *non*-moralized concepts of coercion and exploitation, see Wood (2014, Chapter 12).

In Kant's four examples in the *Groundwork*, what perplexes the agent is whether the duty in question (which is assumed to be *universally* valid) truly applies to *this* action. Issues of judgment about duties are admitted possible. On the topic of suicide, in connection with FH Kant actually *derives* and *formulates* the duty forbidding us to "dispose of the human being in my own person, so as to maim, corrupt or kill him." Then he adds: "The nearer determination of this principle, so as to avoid all misunderstanding, e.g. the amputation of limbs in order to preserve myself, or the risk at which I put my life in order to preserve my life, etc. I must here pass over: they belong to morals proper" (G 4:429). "Morals proper" here means moral *judgment* – the application of general concepts to particular cases. *Suicide* is necessarily wrong, but some courses of action that might result in my death may not be *suicide* – hence not forbidden. Analogous qualifications apply to the other three duties – indeed, to *all* duties.

Kant's taxonomy of duties. Kant divides the four duties he "enumerates" into duties toward oneself/duties toward others and perfect duties/imperfect duties. As we've seen, he postpones until the *Metaphysics of Morals* his account of the taxonomy involved (G 4:421 n, MM 6:390–391). But it will profit us to look at that account before taking up his two examples of imperfect duties.

Toward oneself/toward others. For Kant, the concept of a duty toward (*gegen*) someone is not a duty to do anything that necessarily *benefits* them. It is instead a duty imposed on the subject of the duty (the *subjectum obligationis*) by the *will* of the one to whom the duty is owed (the *auctor obligationis*). The will of the *auctor* need not be self-serving. In the case of a duty to others, the will of the person toward whom I have the duty imposes the duty, so that for many duties, this person can release me from the duty at their discretion; even when the duty is one from which I may not be released, the will of the other is involved in administering the duty – the person may consent to certain ways of my fulfilling the duty and not to others. The authority of one person to impose a duty on another is based on the humanity (as end in itself) of the *auctor obligationis*. In the case of duties to oneself, it is oneself as a rational (noumenal) being imposing a duty on oneself as a (phenomenal) being on whom the duty is imposed (MM 6:417–418).[17]

Perfect/imperfect. This terminology was devised by Pufendorf, and used by Thomasius, Sulzer, Mendelssohn, and others. It originally distinguished *perfect* duties, duties to do or omit specific actions and at the same time duties that may be coercively enforced, from *imperfect* duties that may not be coerced. Kant is consciously revising this "terminology of the schools" based on the entirely sound point that there could be duties to do or omit specific actions that may not be coercively enforceable because they are *ethical* and not *juridical* duties. It is to this class of strict or unexceptionable *ethical* duties that Kant now wants to apply the term 'perfect duty.' But he puts it this way: "I understand by a perfect duty that which permits no exception to the advantage of inclination" (G 4:421 n). Where does this formulation leave the concept of *imperfect* duty? Is an imperfect duty one that *does* admit of exceptions in the interest of inclination? Such a category seems to make no sense in Kant's theory, since (as we've just seen) any duty involves a moral concept: obligatory, forbidden, or meritorious. It would be self-contradictory to say of a class of actions that they are obligatory and yet there might be exceptions in the interest of inclination. 'Exceptions' could mean only that an action might be thought obligatory but is not (e.g. keeping a promise made under duress to do something in itself wrong). That action is not a duty at all. Besides, the whole point of Kant's discussion of the

---

[17] Obviously, here the phenomenal/noumenal distinction has no metaphysical import: it marks two different *ways of thinking about* the very same (rational, embodied) moral agent, or two different *roles* the agent plays in the volitional relation of imposing obligations on itself. The *auctor obligationis* must be a being with the rational capacity to exercise these acts of volition, and also a finite or sensible rational being, with whom I can have empirical acquaintance with its administration of the obligation. This shows why we cannot have duties *toward* (*gegen*), but only duties *in regard to* (*in Ansehung auf*) such entities as non-rational animals, the beauties of nature, and God. These duties seem (by an "amphiboly of moral concepts of reflection") to be duties *toward* these other entities, but they must be duties toward ourselves, since we are the only ones with the capacity, and in the position, to impose the obligation on ourselves (MM 6:442–443).

four examples is that mere inclination ("I don't want to," "I just don't feel like it") *never* suffices to exempt you from any genuine duty. We will see presently that this holds *especially* of the third and fourth examples, involving imperfect duties.

Based on what Kant says later in the *Metaphysics of Morals*, an imperfect duty seems to be what he there calls a 'wide' or 'meritorious' duty, or more specifically, a "duty of virtue" (MM 6:384–395).[18] A duty of virtue is a duty to set certain (kinds of) ends: specifically, (instances of) one's own perfection and the happiness of others (MM 6:382–387). Kant holds that we have latitude (*latitudo, Spielraum*) in the fulfillment of wide or imperfect duties (MM 6: 390). *Imperfect duties* may best be considered as moral *virtues*, just as their opposites are explicitly described by Kant as 'vices' (MM 6: 428–437, 458–461, 465–468). The relation between duty and virtue in Kant is this: sometimes it is contrary to duty not to display a virtue or to display the contrary vice. Other times it is meritorious to display a virtue but not blameworthy not to display it. More specifically, it is virtuous to have some instances of the obligatory ends (duties of virtue) among one's ends, and virtuous to promote these ends in the right ways; it would be vicious and blameworthy not to have any of those kinds of ends, or to have contrary ends, or not to promote the obligatory ends in cases where you definitely should promote them.

Accordingly, perhaps the best way to understand Kant's formulation of the perfect/imperfect distinction in the *Groundwork* is this: We may blamelessly omit some (meritorious) actions, perhaps even in the interest of inclination.[19] That would be how imperfect

---

[18] Not all wide duties are duties of virtue. Specifically, the duty to act from the motive of duty, which is a duty to appraise one's actions in a certain way, and also to strive to be the sort of person for whom the motive of duty is sufficient, is a wide or meritorious duty, but it's not a duty of virtue, because it concerns only what is *formal* in the determination of the will, whereas *duties of virtue* are *material*: they are duties to set certain ends (MM 6:383).

[19] But this is not entirely clear either. Kant says that a wide duty "is not a permission to make exceptions to the maxim of action but only a permission to limit one maxim of duty by another (e.g. love of one's neighbor in general by love of one's parents" (MM 6:390)). However, it seems consistent with this to say that one may, without making exceptions to a *maxim* of duty (e.g. love of one's neighbor), omit

duty fits Kant's formulation at G 4:421 n. Conduct promoting obligatory ends is always meritorious, omitting such conduct not blameworthy – *except* in cases where conduct fails to display sufficient commitment to the obligatory ends, and then it is vicious, blameworthy, and even while falling under the heading of imperfect duty, it violates a strict duty. Kant's third and fourth examples are supposed to illustrate such cases.

Matters of degree, matters of circumstance. There are clear indications that the perfect/imperfect (or narrow/wide) distinction is less like a strict dichotomy than it is like a continuum, or perhaps even a multi-dimensional map. Some actions promoting obligatory ends (imperfect duties) can be more binding (closer to perfect duties) than others (MM 6:390). Circumstances and relationships may also play a role in determining when and how far we might be obligated. For instance, it may be more obligatory to aid your parents than your neighbor, and more obligatory, *ceteris paribus*, to aid a person in greater need than one in lesser need. We have seen that it might be an excessive 'purism' or 'pedantry' "regarding the wideness of the obligation" to regard some duties too strictly (MM 6:426). In fact, if we look closely, we see that most of Kant's Casuistical Questions involve some issues regarding the *degree* to which an imperfect duty might approach or recede from requiring or forbidding particular actions, and how this might vary under particular *circumstances* (see MM 6:428, 431, 434, 437, 454). Kant's accounts of our various duties (including accounts of virtues and vices) also frequently deal with variations among circumstances, and how a moral agent ought to react to them.

That Kant takes up these issues in Casuistical Questions suggests that he regards the degree of perfection or imperfection involved in

some *actions* that would benefit one's neighbor, and omit them simply in the interest of one's inclinations, not necessarily because one has another duty (e.g. toward one's parents). This seems the only way to accommodate two of Kant's positions: *first*, that we have a standing permission (though not a duty) to pursue our own happiness whenever no duty forbids it (MM 6:388, 451), and also *second*, that there are some actions that are morally indifferent, neither forbidden nor required (MM 6:409).

a duty as a matter for moral *judgment*, and the way an agent should choose actions falling under a dutiful end or maxim by considering their relation to particular circumstances. This is how Kant's Doctrine of Virtue handles those issues that Aristotle's theory deals with through its doctrine of the mean (NE 1107a–1109b27).[20] We see this in the *Groundwork's* two examples of imperfect duty. They concern cases where an agent is worried about *how morally binding* certain actions are in fulfillment of an imperfect duty, and whether under the circumstances the agent could be exempt from the duty to do these specific actions.

Third example: Letting your talent rust. In this example, the agent "finds in himself a talent, which could, by means of some cultivation, make him into a human being useful for all sorts of aims" (G 4:423). He does not want to take the trouble to develop this particular talent, because it would interfere with his life of pleasure and comfort. But he wonders whether neglecting to develop that talent would be contrary to duty.

Here (and in the fourth example as well) it is essential that the perfection/imperfection of a duty can be a continuum. *How* strict it is can be relative to circumstances, so that some actions falling under the imperfect duty can be more strictly required than others. *This* agent is worried that *for him*, and *for this particular talent*, it might be contrary to duty for him not to develop it. That worry does not arise for just any person or for just any talent. There are all sorts

[20] It is one of the great misfortunes in the history of ethics that Kant apparently never read Aristotle, and knew his ethical theory mainly from a very brief and inadequate presentation of it in Brucker (1742–1744, pp. 835–839). Kant rejects Aristotle's doctrine of the mean because he takes it to hold that a virtuous action is one that combines two vicious principles: courage combines cowardice with rashness; thrift combines miserliness with profligacy (MM 6:406, 432). Obviously this is a grotesque caricature of Aristotle, comparable to the tediously familiar and silly arguments that Kant's ethics is hostile to the emotions or is committed to inhuman moral inflexibility. In fact, Kant's doctrine of virtue has much in common with Aristotle's. Kant also holds that judgment must apply a single principle of virtue – a single imperfect duty – to different circumstances, resulting in issues of judgment regarding whether and how they display certain virtues or vices, and thus whether they are required, permitted, or forbidden.

of things you might be better at than you are, and you might not be acting contrary to duty in not cultivating that particular skill, even if you omitted to do so just because you didn't want to. In the example, therefore, it is important that this talent is somehow special. It must be a talent the agent sees that he has in a special degree, or whose development by him would be especially useful to him or to people around him. For many talents there might be good reasons not to develop them. Given your resources, you might not be able to afford to develop this particular talent (e.g. a talent for judging expensive wines), or you may need to develop mainly those talents that would earn you a living, and be justified in giving them priority over others. We must suppose that none of these reasons apply to the agent in this example. His maxim is simply that he does not want to take the trouble because he wants a life of ease and gratification.

Kant's aim is to use FLN to show why this is not a morally justifiable reason for him to neglect the development of this parti-cular talent. Kant begins by admitting that the agent's maxim passes the contradiction in conception test: a nature is quite con-ceivable in which all rational beings let their talents rust. Kant claims, however, that the agent's maxim does not pass the contra-diction in will test. It is impossible for him to will that his maxim should be a universal law of nature – which Kant seems to think is equivalent to this maxim "being implanted in us as such by a natural instinct." His argument is this: "For as a rational being he necessarily wills that all the faculties in him should be devel-oped, because they are serviceable and given to him for all kinds of possible aims" (G 4:423).

Given what we've just seen, the argument might seem puzzling for two reasons: first, the claim here is no longer about this parti-cular talent, but about *all*; second, it might not be clear how we are to understand the assertion that *as a rational being*, the agent necessarily wills that all his faculties should be developed. To take the second puzzle first: it's clear that the rational volition in question cannot be *morally* motivated. For since the agent is trying to settle a moral issue, to appeal at this point to a morally motivated volition would render the argument redundant and question-begging. Instead, the argument may be appealing to natural teleology, as in the first example: this is suggested by the remark that his faculties are *"given to him* for all kinds of possible aims."* An even better argument, though, would be the following: Since our faculties are "serviceable" for all possible aims, it would not be rational, purely from the standpoint of instrumental rationality, for us to develop *none* of them, hence (in particular) to leave undeveloped even those we have especially compelling reasons to develop. That also explains why Kant mentions *all* talents, even though the issue is this special talent. For the agent's reason (i.e. justification or excuse) for not developing this talent is just that, preferring a life of idleness and enjoyment, he simply *doesn't want to.*[21] But if that excuse were acceptable, it would exempt any person, or all people, from taking the trouble to develop *any talent or faculty whatever.* From this we can see that this maxim (this justification for exempting oneself from the duty to develop this talent) is not one that any rational human being can will, because it conflicts with the necessary volition, based on instrumental reason, that we should develop at least some of our faculties as means to the discretionary ends we set.

Notice once again that the claim from which Kant is arguing is not about what people *do* will or might *in fact* will – perhaps some

---

[21] To focus on Kant's valid point, we need to do our best to put to one side his ignorant, racist suggestion that the South Sea Islanders do this. Kant had even been scolded on this subject by Georg Forster, who knew a lot about these people, and whose views Kant discusses (with disgracefully insufficient sympathy or comprehension) in UTP. Kant's quite defensible idea was better presented in his review of Herder, where (again spoiling it with another ugly derogatory reference to Tahitians) he takes issue with Herder's idea that happiness and contentment constitute our only natural ends. Kant wonders whether, if the human race were to live in this way, "one could give a satisfying answer to the question why they should exist at all, or whether it not have been just as good for an island to be populated with happy sheep and cattle as with human beings who are happy and merely enjoying themselves?" (RH 8:65). Kant could certainly have found members of the European leisure classes of his day whose wasted lives of idleness and luxury would illustrate his point far better than any Tahitians ever could.

people are so irrational that they do not choose to acquire the necessary means to ends they set. The issue is about what it would be *rational* (*instrumentally* rational) for them to will. Willing the means to their ends is what they *must* will in order to be rational; the argument claims that conflicts with what they *would have* to will if they were to will this agent's maxim to be a universal law of nature. Again, the issue is not the agent's maxim simply as a general life-policy, but instead considered as a specific excuse for neglecting the particular talent in question. Although there are many talents the agent might innocently fail to develop, he is supposed to see that if he doesn't develop *this* talent, he is not taking a rational stance toward his existence as a an end-setting rational being. At a deeper level: if he neglects it, that exhibits a self-regarding *vice*: he does not value his rational nature as he should. He violates a duty imposed by his pure reason on his sensibly affected rational nature.

Fourth example: Refusing sympathy and aid to others. In the fourth example too, it is significant that there can be degrees of perfection or imperfection (narrowness or wideness) regarding duties of virtue. The agent in this case is a person "for whom things are going well," who is aware of *specific* others who "have to struggle with great hardships (with which he could well help them)" (G 4:423). The issue is whether *this agent's* helping *these people* falls under the duty of beneficence as it applies to him. This, once again, is an issue of moral *judgment* – of whether the concept of the duty of beneficence applies to this case. And the agent's maxim (or, as Kant calls it, his "way of thinking," *Denkungsart*) gives him what he is tempted to think is a good reason for judging that it does not. The agent's "way of thinking" includes the following four thoughts:

1. What does it have to do with me?
2. I do not wish these people ill. In fact, I *wish* them well.
3. I even respect their rights; I would take nothing from them that is rightfully theirs.
4. But I *don't want* to contribute to their welfare or assistance in time of need. (G 4:423)

The first thought is initially a natural one. For there might be many people in the world who are facing hardships, but no reason why *I* (in particular) should have any duty to help them. I might lack the resources to help them. Even if I have the resources, I may have no clear idea what their needs are, or how my resources could be effective in helping them – especially if they live far away (in Bangladesh, Syria, or the Congo).[22] On the other hand, even (or especially) if the needy people live right down the street, I may not be able to help them in a way they do not experience as embarrassing or even humiliating. For Kant these would all be good reasons why their plight might have *nothing to do with me* – that is, why it might impose no duty *on me in particular.*

As was mentioned earlier, whether or not we approve, it is no part of Kant's ethics to claim that each of us is automatically required (as by some principle of impartial benevolence) to help just anyone on the planet who might need it. Kant's ethics holds that unless impartiality is called for by our role in specific human practices, we are permitted (and we might even be required) to give priority to the needs and interests of our friends, our family, our neighbors. Despite its false reputation (based on disgracefully common misreadings of a single paragraph early in the *Groundwork*), Kantian ethics is an ethics of personal engagement and caring, in which friendship is an important value (see Wood, 2017a). Kant insists on a duty of "sympathetic participation" (*Teilnehmung*) (MM 6:456–457; see Baron, 1991, and Fahmy, 2009). This includes a duty to expose ourselves to the needs of those around us and to empathize with them. This is neither a matter of passive feeling nor of impartial benevolence to all, but rather a duty to reach out and interact, to extend the range of

---

[22] The world is now a much smaller place than it was in Kant's day. We surely do have duties to people far away that Kant – cosmopolitan though he was – could not have acknowledged because he could have known nothing about them. But it is a mistake to think that ethical theories giving primacy to the impartial promotion of welfare are better at taking account of our duties to people far away. Concern with the needy in distant lands might be even worse than indifference if it is uncomprehending or condescending. Widened Kantian sympathetic participation would be far better, both as a trait of our own characters and also for its influence on those we would help.

our emotional involvement with others. This duty specifically involves *partiality* toward those people in whose situation we are able to participate, resulting in an empathy for them that elicits our active caring.

These very considerations, however, would show why in the situation described it is so deeply questionable for the agent to ask, rhetorically, "What does it have to do with me?" For he is described as *seeing* that the others are struggling with hardships, and also *being aware* that he could well help them. In the context of Kantian ethics, these considerations would directly suggest that he has a strict *duty* to help. The agent's maxim (or "way of thinking") is meant to articulate the reasons why he thinks he may nevertheless be exempt from that duty. The last three thoughts listed are meant to defend the first thought: that their plight has *nothing to do with him*. These three thoughts are: *first*, that he bears them no ill will and even wishes them well, *second*, that he does not envy them, or intend to take anything from them that is theirs, and *finally*, there is the clincher: *he does not want to help them*. As in the third example, the target of the argument from FUL is the assumption, involved in some ethical theories, that what ultimately matters is just our empirical desires and attitudes (whether selfish or other-directed).

Kant again admits that this way of thinking could pass the contradiction in conception test. He even thinks a world in which it held as a universal law of nature would be a *better* world than one in which people talk about sympathy and beneficence, and even occasionally practice them, but also cheat and violate people's rights whenever they can get away with it. (Kant doubtless thinks this world is our actual world.) He now again denies that the agent's way of thinking can pass the contradiction in will test. "For a will that resolved on this would conflict with itself, since the case could sometimes arise in which he needs the love and sympathetic participation (*Teilnehmung*) of others, and where, through such a natural law arising from his own will, he would rob himself of all the hope of assistance that he wishes for himself" (G 4:423).

The argument is this: Whether or not this well-to-do agent ever does in fact need the love and sympathy of others, if somebody stood to *him* in the same relation that he stands to the people he sees in need, it would be contrary to reason – that is, it would conflict with a necessary rational volition of his – if he did not will that that person sympathize with and help him. It would not be rational for him to accept as an excuse that that person bears him no ill will, does not violate his rights, and just does not happen to want to help him. Once again, the rationality here, on pain of vicious circularity or redundancy, could not be moral. I suggest that in the fourth example it is best understood as *prudential*: based on our rational desire for our own happiness. That is, it would be prudentially irrational for any human being to be so sure he could do without the sympathy and aid of others that he could will (i.e. rationally choose) that they refuse him sympathy and help if he were in need.

Perhaps these are controversial claims about what it is rational to will. Rugged individualists might claim that pride in one's independence takes rational precedence even over one's needs, so that the stubborn refusal ever to ask for charity from anyone provides a sufficient reason why a person might rationally make the very choices Kant considers contrary to reason. Kant is not unsympathetic to this point of view. He is sensitive to the way taking charity from others humiliates you; he thinks you even have a duty to yourself to avoid being in a position of needing it (MM 4:436, 459). He thinks that a cold, unsympathizing temperament, if combined with the fortitude to make you endure hardship, would make a person "not nature's worst product" (G 4:399); but not nature's best product either. More to the point: it is one thing to say that you should try not to need help from others, and a very different thing to say that if you are successful in that trying, it excuses you from giving help to those who truly do need it – especially if you are well off, see their need, and are aware you can help them. In such a case, you'd be trying to use your rugged individualism as merely an excuse for your arrogant inhumanity. As before, however, the question we ought to be asking is not whether we agree with either Kant's premises or his conclusions, but rather whether, by way of FLN, the conclusions follow if we grant the premises. I think we can see already that they do.

Even if Kant's premises here may be disputed, he holds some other views that support them. First, he thinks that it is true of the human condition generally that people are interdependent. However independent they should try to be, all human beings do need the help, and especially the love (both the sympathetic participation that gives rise to sympathetic feeling, and the principled benevolent action) of others. "Our self-love cannot be separated from our need to be loved (helped in case of need) by others in turn" (MM 6:393). Second, as Kant understands it, "sympathetic participation" (*Teilnehmung*) requires mutual communication and sharing with others of our thoughts and feelings (MM 6: 456–457, 471). Kant holds that no human creature can be happy without receiving sympathetic participation from others. In this fourth example, however, the agent is portrayed as truly doing well. So he must already be receiving from some others the very sympathetic participation he now proposes to deny to those he knows need it from him. From these considerations it is clear that the way of thinking he offers as the excuse for his indifference to their needs is not one he could rationally will everyone to take, especially in their conduct toward him.

Once again we see that FLN is *not* being used as a general test for the permissibility of whatever maxims we might happen to bring to it based on our inclinations or prudential reason. It is a canon of judgment for applying an already recognized general duty. The tests are restricted to the situation of *this* agent, dealing with a specific moral tension arising from this duty and his temptation to exempt himself from it. They show this agent that his proposed excuse for refusing aid and sympathy to *these* people does not stand the test of universal reason.

Third Part: The Other Formulas

§7. The Formula of Humanity

What is an end in itself? FH is grounded on a kind of *value* or *end* – humanity or rational nature in persons, as *end in itself*. As we've already mentioned, 'humanity' in this context refers to our capacity to govern our lives by setting ends according to reason. It is controversial in the literature how far what is to be regarded as an end in itself involves also *personality* – the specifically moral capacity of human beings.[23] But basic to Kant's principle is the thought that the end in question is not any state of affairs, but a being – the *person him- or herself*. It may be something we can conclude from a person's being an end in itself that we should value certain states of affairs – for instance, the person's continued existence or their well-being. But it is the *person* who is the end in itself. Some philosophers question whether this use of the concept of 'end' is odd, technical, or even nonsensical.[24] That wrongheaded puzzlement exhibits the deplorable corruption perpetrated against moral philosophy by shallow consequentialist theories that locate all value in states of affairs. In the most general sense of the term, an *end* (*Zweck*) is simply anything *for whose sake* (in German: *um ... deswillen*) we do act or should act. When we act for the sake of a person's survival or happiness, we also – *and more fundamentally* – act *for the sake of the person*. Persons are *always* more properly ends than are any states of affairs, and most states of affairs that are ends are ends only because of some person or persons who are the more fundamental ends on which these other ends are based.

Sometimes people discussing Kant's philosophy in English speak of the end in itself by saying that I am an end in *myself* ... you are an end in *yourself* ... he or she is an end in *himself* or *herself*. This talk says something true, even something important, because of course it *is* the *person* who is the end. But it also says something rather obvious and superficial, and it obscures the crucial point. It definitely *misunderstands* what Kant meant by the phrase *Zweck an sich selbst*. If he had meant this phrase to refer merely to the *person* who is the end, he would have said in German: *Zweck an mir selbst ... dir selbst ... ihm selbst ... ihr selbst*; but these are not expressions he ever uses. *Zweck*

---

[23] For a defense of the claim that it does, see, for example, Allison (2011, Chapter 8). For a contrasting view, see Wood (1999, pp. 118–122), and Wood (2008, pp. 88–92).

[24] "Can a person *be* my purpose? No. The question makes no grammatical sense" (Wolff, 1972, p. 175).

an sich selbst should always be translated 'end in *it*self.' It refers not to *what* or *who* the end is, but instead to the special *kind of end* that persons are.

We set certain objects or states of affairs as ends. Kant calls that an end to be effected (*zu bewirkenden Zweck*) as contrasted with existent or self-sufficient ends (*selbständigen Zwecken*) that is, *persons* for whose sake we act (G 4:437). My ends to be effected are also discretionary (*beliebigen*) ends. That is the concept contrasting directly with *end in itself.* When I set an end, I am rationally required (by instrumental reason) to employ means to achieve it. But discretionary ends are rationally binding on us (through instrumental reason) only to the extent that we actually set them. (This is true even of ends duty requires us to set.) If I had not set the end, or if I later abandon it (at my discretion) or subordinate it (again, at my discretion) to other discretionary ends, then the basic norm of instrumentally rationality, while still universally valid, no longer applies *to me in this case.* Suppose I make it my end to write a book about Rousseau. If I later lose interest in my Rousseau project and put in place of it the end of writing a book about Marx, then I am no longer bound by instrumental reason to write about Rousseau. Ends in themselves, however, are not like that. We are *categorically* required to act for their sake. Persons always have a rational claim on us as ends irrespective of our inclinations or discretionary choices. That is what it means to say that they are *objective* ends. That is why persons alone, as *ends in themselves*, can ground obedience to categorical imperatives.

Regarded as a formula of the categorical imperative – a determinate way of solving a specific problem (CPrR 5:8 n) – the problem FH is specifically assigned to solve is: *For what determining ground (Bestimmungsgrund) or motive (Bewegungsgrund) could someone obey a categorical imperative?* The concept 'end in itself' provides the only conceivable solution to this problem (G 4:427–428). The identification of humanity in persons as the sole end in itself tells us what in particular that ground or motive is. As we will see presently, FH is also assigned a further problem: that of grounding specific general ethical duties, such as the four used in Kant's illustrations.

Humanity is an end in itself – an objective value which, wherever it is found in persons, makes unconditional claims on us. But Kant also ascribes to humanity – or more precisely, to personality – a *dignity*: a supreme and incomparable worth. In contrast to the value of entities having mere price, the worth of beings with dignity may not be traded away or sacrificed for anything, not even for something else having dignity (G 4:434–435).[25] Technically, in Kant's theory it is *humanity* – the capacity to set ends through reason – that is an *end in itself*; it is *personality*, the human capacity to obey objective moral laws of which the person can regard him- or herself as the legislator, that has *dignity*. But humanity and personality in these technical senses are necessarily co-extensive.[26] So Kant also justifiably says that *persons* are ends in themselves and that *humanity* has dignity.

What is it to treat a person as an end in itself? FH issues to you the categorical imperative that you should always act for the sake of the humanity or rational nature in persons. In other words, you must "*act so that you treat humanity, as much in your own person as in the person of every other, always as an end and never merely as a means*" (G 4:429). What sort of conduct does this command?

One strategy philosophers have employed in interpreting it could be described as the *analytical* or *criterial* strategy. They analyze or clarify the concept 'treating humanity as an end in itself' by setting forth a more precise account of the kinds of behavior that count as doing this and not doing it. This is how we might clarify other concepts we find troublesome because they are vague or

---

[25] This characterization of dignity, however, is merely negative. I suggest that its positive meaning is that persons, as self-governing beings, are never to be valued merely as objects in some calculation carried out by others – for example, paternalistic Wolffian cameralists or utilitarian social engineers who claim the right to decide for others what their good consists in and how it is to be pursued. See Wood (2014, pp. 65–69), and Wood (2016, pp. 200–250).

[26] Some think that Kant is denying this at R 6:26n. But all he is saying there is that humanity and personality are different *concepts*. His inference from freedom in the negative sense to freedom in the positive sense entails that they are co-extensive (G 4:446–447; cf. CPrR 5:33). For discussion of this point, see Wood (1999, pp. 364–366, n. 11).

unclear. For instance, take the concepts 'book' and 'article.' Someone who divides their bibliography into books and articles might be troubled by these Cambridge Elements, because they are too long to be articles, but too short to be books. So they might set forth criteria (e.g. numbers of pages, numbers of words) clarifying each of these concepts. That might or might not solve their bibliographical problem, but whatever interest led them to establish criteria for the distinction, they would presumably have reasons for the criteria they laid down. These reasons, however, would be presupposed, not furnished, by the specification of the criteria. Criterial accounts necessarily defer the rational justification for the criteria to arguments these criteria by themselves cannot in principle provide.

Such a criterial account has sometimes been given for FH, by saying that to treat a person as end in itself means to respect the person's rights, to consider the person's aims and welfare, and so on. One difficulty here is that no possible analysis will ever be complete. But some philosophers have adopted this procedure because they have thought that this is the only thing you can do with FH. This approach is fine for those who like the rhetorical sound of FH but have no inkling of its role in Kant's ethical theory and remain utterly oblivious to the problems that FH, as a *formula*, is supposed to solve. In the context of the *Groundwork*, humanity as end in itself is supposed to solve the problem of identifying the *rational ground for obeying categorical imperatives* and also the problem of *deriving the content of ethical duties*. Both problems involve *explaining why* people should be treated in some ways and not in other ways. No merely analytical or criterial account could do that.

What is it about persons that gives them the value: *end in itself?* Above it was argued that Kant regards every human being as attributing worth as end in itself to him- or herself simply on the ground that in making choices, I necessarily ascribe to myself the authority to direct my own life. Kant argues that in acknowledging that others are *free*, I commit myself to ascribe the same value to them (G 4:429, 448). This value belongs just as much to bad people as to good people. The nature of this value depends on how we think of the capacity to direct one's own life. Above I suggested that its foundation is that every rational being must be treated fundamentally as a co-deliberator in matters affecting them. That means we must all be a party to answering the questions: 'What is this humanity or rational nature that is an end in itself?' and 'What does it mean that it is an end in itself?' We are all conversation partners in the enterprise of exploring and developing the meaning of these concepts.

Ronald Dworkin argues that moral concepts generally are *not criterial but interpretive concepts* (see Dworkin, 2011, Part Two). He is absolutely right, and this applies especially to the crucial Kantian concept "end in itself." The true nature of the reasons why we should treat rational nature in persons as an end in itself can be brought out only through a *hermeneutical approach*, in which we interpret behavior, coming to understand some behavior as *respectful* or *caring* as regards the value of humanity in persons, and other behavior as *disrespectful* or *uncaring*. As I understand Kant, this is his approach in ethics, as it is Aristotle's (NE 1094b15–1095a2). One sign of this is just the importance of judgment in Kant's ethics, which I have been stressing. Judgment marks the inherent limitations of an analytical or criterial, hence discursive-deductive approach to moral reasoning. I think it is clear that Kant does adopt such an interpretive or hermeneutical approach to the application of FH. FH is by far the formula to which Kant most often appeals when grounding his claims about duties (both perfect and imperfect), virtues, and vices in his Doctrine of Virtue. Kant specifies under FH the four duties that were earlier merely "enumerated" and applied by judgment through FLN. We *derive* them by seeing how kinds of conduct do or do not treat humanity in persons as an end in itself:[27]

---

[27] For more on this, see Wood (1999, 135–155, 323–325). Another way (not made explicit in Kant) that we could relate Kant's derivation of duties from FH to his theory of judgment is to regard the various concepts of duty as resulting from acts of *reflective* judgment. We reflect on the manifold of acts, ends, and attitudes that might pertain to conduct conforming to or violating FH, and

Perfect duty to oneself (suicide): "The human being, however, is not a thing, hence not something that can be used *merely* as a means, but must in all his actions always be considered as an end in itself. Thus I cannot dispose of the human being in my own person, so as to maim, corrupt or kill him" (G 4:429).

Perfect duty to others (the false promise): "As rational beings . . . persons ought always to be esteemed at the same time as ends, i.e. only as beings who have to be able to contain in themselves the end of precisely the same action" (G 4:430).

Imperfect duty to oneself (developing this talent): "It is not enough that the action does not conflict with humanity in our person as end in itself, it must also *harmonize with it*. Now in humanity there are predispositions to greater perfection, which belong to ends of nature in regard to the humanity in our subject; to neglect these would at most be able to subsist with the *preservation* of humanity as end in itself, but not with the *furthering* of this end" (G 4:430).

Imperfect duty to others (providing aid and sympathetic participation): "The natural end that all human beings have is their own happiness. Now humanity would be able to subsist if no one contributed to the happiness of others, yet did not intentionally remove anything from it; only this is only a negative and not a positive agreement with *humanity as end in itself*, if everyone does not aspire, as much as he can, to further the ends of others. For regarding the subject which is an end in itself: if that representation is to have its *total* effect on me, then its ends must as far as possible also be *my* ends" (G 4:430).

The inexhaustible meaning of *humanity as end in itself*. Humanity or rational nature, as it is found in persons, is something about which we are constantly learning: through the sciences, at least when they escape superficiality and reductiveness in dealing with our nature, but perhaps at least as much through the arts.

thereby we form the various concepts of perfect and imperfect duty that enable the manifold of certain acts to be grasped in one consciousness – the concept of that specific general duty. I regard this as an intriguing and plausible suggestion about how duties are derived from FH, but I don't propose to explore it further here.

We are studying our humanity, or at least we should be studying it, in all branches of philosophy; it is also the chief object with which religions deal – even if they are unaware that all thoughts and feelings directed toward God are really thoughts and feelings that have humanity as their object.[28]

To come to understand or interpret the meaning of humanity is at the same time to come to understand its value as end in itself. For the two are the same. This, like the Aristotelian concepts of happiness and virtue, is the fundamental point where facts and values cannot come apart. This is why Fichte spoke of the *Bestimmung des Menschen* – the *determination* or nature, at the same time the *vocation* – that belongs to each of us as a human being and to our entire species. What we are is inseparable from the ethical value found in us, and also inseparable from our deliberations about what we ought to be, even if we always fall far short of what we ought to be.

Moral progress since Kant's day consists in our changing understandings about all these matters. The changes are most conspicuous regarding commonality-in-diversity of cultures and races, in the equality of men and women, in the deepening appreciation of the importance and variability of sexuality in human life, and perhaps most of all, the relations of our absurdly rare and anomalous species – the only rational, self-comprehending, and self-directing species we now have any reason to believe exists anywhere – to the vastness of nature surrounding it, and equally to its own precarious and self-endangered future. Just as Kant could not have anticipated these developments, so this progress can be expected to go on indefinitely in the future in ways that no one can predict.

The ever-widening and ever-deepening interpretive appropriation of the meaning of reason and humanity, and its application to Kant's FH, is an endlessly rich historical task set by and for the entire human species. Here we must bring our (brief and inadequate) discussion of it to an abrupt close, but the meaning of the

---

[28] As Fichte was perhaps the first to realize. See Fichte (2011, p. 41), and Wood (2016, pp. 18–19, 36–37,195–196, 248–250).

claim that humanity is an end in itself is in fact a literally inexhaustible topic.

§8. Autonomy and the Realm of Ends

FA is the combination of FUL/FLN and FH. It is the complete and most definitive statement of the supreme principle of morality. Where FUL/FLN offers a canon of judgment, presupposing but not grounding determinate duties, and FH grounds an indefinite plurality of duties and moral evaluations, FA states the law itself to which the rational will is subject. FA is also the formula that receives the most varied statements. These begin with: "the idea of every rational being as a will giving universal law" (G 4:431) but concentrate on formulations involving the thought that there are certain maxims that contain in themselves the volition that they be universal laws, and FA is the positive command to follow those maxims (G 4:432, 437–438, 440, 447). This same thought is also expressed in the formulations of FH found in Kant's other ethical works, using the term *gelten* (to hold, count, or be valid): "So act that the maxim of your will could always hold (*gelten*) at the same time as a principle giving universal law" (CPrR 5:30). "Act upon a maxim that can also hold (*gelten*) as a universal law" (MM 6:225). Kant uses related terminology in the *Groundwork* when he says: "Act on a maxim that at the same time contains in itself its own universal validity (*Gültigkeit*) for every rational being" (G 4:437–438).

How FA differs from FUL/FLN. Many statements of FA sound similar to statements of FUL. But there is a crucial difference. FUL tells you to ask about your maxim whether it *can* (without contradiction in conception or contradiction in the will) be both thought and willed as a universal law; if it cannot be, then it is impermissible to act on it. But the question FA asks is different. The property of a maxim after which it inquires is a far stronger one: Does this maxim *hold* – that is, is it actually *valid* – as a universal law? Does it *include in itself the rational volition* that it be such a law? If it does, then as a matter of rational volition, it does actually make itself a law and therefore holds (*gilt*) as a law. There might well be maxims that pass the test proposed by FUL, and thus qualify (though perhaps only conditionally and hypothetically) as morally *permissible*. But a maxim that passes the test proposed by FA *actually makes itself* a universal law and *is actually valid* as such a law. It not only might be *permissible* to act on such a maxim, but you are *categorically required* to act on it. In the *Critique of Practical Reason*, this special self-legislating property of a maxim is given a new name: "legislative form" (CPrR 5:27).

In FUL/FLN, and also in many statements of FA, there is a modal component: *possibility*. But its meaning in the two formulas is strikingly different. FUL (FLN) asks you whether you *can* think and also will your maxim to be a universal law (or law of nature). The 'can' here means: the maxim passes a certain test involving what you *can* think and will without contradiction or conflicting volitions. But FA commands you positively to act on maxims that *can hold* as universal laws or *can make themselves into* universal laws. These maxims not merely can but *do actually* hold as laws. Here the 'can' is included only because there is a distinction between two kinds of principles: maxims (subjective principles) and laws (objective principles) (G 4:400 n, CPrR 5:19). No maxim (no merely subjective principle, as such) *actually is* an objective law. At most it *can* be such a law, if it meets certain conditions: namely, having legislative form or including in itself the rational volition that it be a law. But some maxims, as regards their *content*, actually do have legislative form: they *do* will themselves to be such laws, and so they *do* hold or *are actually* valid as universal laws. They don't merely pass a *sine qua non* test of permissibility. Their legislative form makes them *actual universal laws*, such as FA positively commands us to follow.

We have seen that each *formula* of the moral law is called a 'formula' because it precisely solves a specific problem (CPrR 5:8 n). The first specific problem the formula FA is assigned is that of summarizing the other formulas, and providing a complete statement of the moral law. In the Third Section of the *Groundwork*, through its relation to the presupposition that the rational will is free, FA also solves the specific problem of providing a deduction of the moral law as a whole, thereby also showing that everyday morality is after all not an illusion (G 4:448–463).

There is no thinkability-willability test for legislative form. Kant's examples of FUL (G 4:402) and FLN (G 4:421–424) offer us universalizability as a standard of judgment we can use to decide whether a maxim provides an acceptable reason for exempting an agent from a specific duty in a specific case. If there were a universalizability test for legislative form, then FA would indeed be what many philosophers think a moral principle must be *for*: It would be a principle or criterion we could directly apply in deciding what to do and providing a discursive reasoning procedure for such decisions. I think many of Kant's readers in effect treat FUL/FLN as if it were something like a test for legislative form – or, realizing reluctantly that it cannot be a test for that, as a test for the *permissibility* of whatever maxim might be brought before it. Above I have tried to show how that is a mistaken interpretation of how Kant thinks FUL/FLN are to be used. There is no test we can apply to determine regarding any given maxim whether it has legislative form. Kant never proposes such a test or makes use of one.

It is precisely because FA *does not* offer us anything like a criterion or procedure for determining right and wrong action that Kant's three formulas of the moral law are structured as they are. Moral agents must decide what to do by considering a set of duties (perfect and imperfect) (grounded on FH), and devising a course of life in which these duties figure as essential components. Then (with the help of FUL/FLN) they must apply these duties in specific situations through judgment. FA/FRE merely summarizes all this in the form of a single categorical imperative.

In the *Critique of Practical Reason*, Kant argues that we can see directly that certain maxims could *not* have legislative form. These are "material practical principles" – namely, those arising from an independent desire for an object (CPrR 5:21). They could not be laws because the independent (empirical) ground for their rational appeal to us disqualifies them from being categorical imperatives. That is why practical laws must be such on account of their legislative form, not on account of their matter (CPrR 5:22). Practical laws rest on an objective end (humanity as end in itself, but this is not an end anyone sets, but an existent or self-sufficient end) (CPrR 5:87). Practical laws also command us to *set* certain (kinds of) ends: our own perfection and the happiness of others (MM 6: 382–388). But these ends are *subsequent* to the laws, not their ground (CPrR 5:62–63).

Kant also thinks we can tell *immediately* (that is, *not* through any process of reasoning or by any general criterion or "CI-Procedure") that certain maxims not only do not have legislative form but even conflict with FA and with maxims having legislative form. He gives two examples:

> *vengeance*: "Let no insult pass unavenged" (CPrR 5:19).[29]
>
> *greedy avarice*: "Increase my wealth by every safe means" (CPrR 5:27).[30]

But Kant never suggests that we can tell immediately for just *any* maxim whether it has legislative form, lacks legislative form, or conflicts with maxims having legislative form. Consider all the maxims that might be possible answers to these following questions: *Which* insults may be permissibly avenged? If so, which kinds of vengeance might be permissible in response to which insults? *How* is it morally permissible to respond to an insult? (There is no general answer to these questions; the right way to respond to insults always depends on good judgment about particular circumstances.) Or again: By precisely *which* safe means it is morally permissible and impermissible to increase your wealth? By all *legal* means? Are some

---

[29] *Nemo me impune lacessit* ["No one provokes me with impunity"] was the family motto of the house of Montresor in Edgar Allan Poe's gruesome story *The Casque of Amontillado*. It was also the family motto of the house of Stuart, which ruled England for most of the seventeenth century. It is a motto common among tyrants.

[30] *Greedy* avarice, a violation of a duty to others, is distinct from *miserly* avarice, which violates a duty to ourselves (MM 6:432). Kant illustrates greedy avarice with the clandestine conversion of a deposit left with me in trust (CPrR 5:27; cf. TP 8:286). Notice that this is only a special case of the impermissible maxim of greedy avarice. In Kant's argument that if converting the deposit were made a universal law then there would be no deposits FUL is being used as a standard of judgment to show why *this instance* of the maxim of greedy avarice is impermissible.

legal means morally forbidden? Which ones? If some philosophers
think some "CI-Procedure" can infallibly answer these questions,
Kant is wise enough not to be among them.

There is also *one* duty that Kant thinks we can derive simply using
the concept of legislative form. This is the duty that we must include
the happiness of others (of *all* others) *somewhere* among our ends. His
reasoning is that, based on the fundamental (non-moral) principle of
prudential reason, everyone necessarily has their own happiness
among their ends. Therefore, the maxim: "I will to include my own
happiness among my ends," is one that all human beings necessarily
adopt insofar as they are rational. But we can give this maxim legislative form, turning it into a maxim that contains the volition that it be
a universal law and therefore that actually holds as a universal law, by
including the happiness of all other rational beings, along with our
own, among our ends. That makes this universal form of our maxim of
self-love into a practical law (CPrR 5:25, MM 6:393, 451). But this duty
is *unique* in that respect. There is no other maxim of prudence such
that every finite rational being necessarily wills it. So this is the *only*
case where we can find a maxim that applies universally to all of us
and then transform it into a universal law (or give it legislative form)
just by expanding the end it sets so that it includes the same end with
respect to all other rational beings.

The realm of ends. It is appropriate to conclude an account of the
system of formulas, as Kant himself does, with FRE. It is the most
definitive formula of all, the A (alpha) and the Ω (omega) of all ethics
as Kant understands it. Regarded as a *formula*, the problem it solves
is to summarize in the form of a moral command the rational answer
to the question: "How shall human beings live together?"

In the phrase *Reich der Zwecke*, the term *Reich* (*realm* or *kingdom* –
a more accurate if anachronistic translation would be *common-
wealth*) actually refers to two distinct but related things. First, it refers
to the "systematic combination" of all *rational beings* in an ideal
community, where each and every one is treated by all others as an
end (an *end in itself*, following FH). Second, it refers to the whole of all
ends to be effected, all the ends set by each and every one of the
rational beings belonging to this community. In reference to this

collection of ends, the term *Reich* says that *these ends* ought to stand in "systematic connection" (G 4:433). The ends of all members of this community must be mutually supportive or cooperative and not in conflict or competition. In this way they should be analogous to the purposive functions of the organs of a living thing. They are even supposed to be a system of *shared* ends, like the common ends by which, in Kant's account of friendship, friends unite their separate happiness or well-being, so that the good of both friends is "swallowed up" into a single common end through "generous mutual love" (MM 6:469; cf. L-Eth-Vigilantius 27:675–685). The realm of ends is an ideal community in which every rational being would be the *friend* of all others. Kant, along with Aristotle, is the moral philosopher for whom *friendship* is the highest value for all practical reason (see Wood, 2017a). FRE is thus a more intuitive way of representing the system of moral laws (the system of maxims with legislative form) referred to by FA. FA commands those laws whose obedience by all rational beings would create a realm of ends. Kantian ethics gives absolute priority to *relationships* between persons, on equal terms, through the sharing and unifying of their ends. Kantian ethics commands this harmony even if it might involve a sacrifice of total utility.

FRE is the A (alpha) of Kantian ethics in the sense that it is in effect the very first formula to be presented by Kant in a published work: *The Critique of Pure Reason*. There Kant sets forth the idea of a "moral world" as "a *corpus mysticum* of the rational beings in [such a world], insofar as their free choice under moral laws has thoroughgoing systematic unity in itself as well as with the freedom of everyone else" (A808/B836). FRE is also the Ω (omega) of Kant's ethics. It is the final and most complete formula Kant presents in the *Groundwork*. It explains how the third formula constitutes the "complete determination" of the moral law (G 4:436). If the realm of ends is the "moral world," then FRE also connects the moral law with Kant's concept of the highest good (*summum bonum*) which represents the final end of the entire world, and plays a key role in Kant's thinking about the connection between morality and religious faith in all three critiques (CPR A795–831/B823–859, CPrR 5: 110–148, CJ 5:425–474). This is also the end that unites the "ethical community" (or "church") – "a loving union of hearts" through which, by sharing and systematically uniting their ends, human beings may promote the moral progress of the species and gradually approach a "kingdom of God on earth" (Rel 6:96–136).

Fourth Part: The Relations among the Formulas

§9. *The Division of Labor among the Formulas*

Each of Kant's three main formulas of the moral law has a specific job, or set of jobs, that cannot be done by any of the others. FUL/FLN provides a "canon of judgment." FH provides the sole motivation (the ground or reason) for obedience to a categorical imperative. It also rationally grounds or justifies, through an interpretive or hermeneutical employment of the idea of an end in itself, and of rational nature or humanity as such an end, the system of ethical duties of which Kant's Doctrine of Virtue provides a philosophical taxonomy. FA/FRE combines in itself the first two formulas, providing the complete and definitive statement of the moral law. FA is used in the Third Section of the *Groundwork* in the deduction of the law through its relation to freedom (G 4:446–455). In the form of FRE, the third formula relates the moral law to Kant's philosophy as a whole, to the conceptions of the moral world, the highest good, the final end of creation itself and the shared goal of the entire human species. These functions of the different formulas cannot be exchanged. None of the formulas can do what any of the others can do.

Are the formulas "equivalent"? The claim that Kant's formulas are "equivalent" is nearly ubiquitous in the literature on Kant's ethics and on the *Groundwork*. It is often stated as if it were a direct report of something Kant had explicitly asserted. But Kant never says any such thing. I think the "equivalence" claim is either obviously false or else hopelessly confused. People should stop making it.

We have just seen that each formula is assigned a distinct function (or set of functions). In that fairly obvious sense, the formulas are *not* "equivalent." Further, the formulas form a *system* (G 4:436). For Kant, a system is a unity, but it is the unity of a *manifold* organized under an *idea* (CPR A832/B860). There could be no *system* consisting of interchangeable (or in that sense, "equivalent") parts or elements. The closest Kant ever comes to saying that the formulas are "equivalent" is that they are "so many formulas of the very same law, one of which of itself unites the other two in itself" (G 4:436). Above we have seen which *one* of the formulas uniquely performs this unifying function: FA/FRE unites FUL/FLN with FH (G 4:431).[31]

Why do people say so confidently that it is Kant's position that the formulas are "equivalent" when in fact he says nothing of the kind? My guess is this: They are taking for granted the idea that a moral principle must provide a procedure through which, in conjunction with a set of non-moral facts, we can reach justified decisions about what we should do. If the different formulas told us to do different things, then they could not be formulas of *the very same law*. Therefore, if they are *formulas of the very same law* then what each of them tells us to do must be exactly the same as what each of the others tells us to do. In that case, however, the formulas would have to be (extensionally) *equivalent*: that is, each would tell us to do exactly the same things as any other would tell us to do. I think this must be how people get from the thing Kant says – that these are "so many formulas of the very same law" – to the thing he *never* says: that they are *equivalent*. But this reasoning rests on a false assumption

---

[31] In many English translations, the passage just quoted *(... deren die eine die anderen zwei von selbst in sich vereinigt)* is inaccurately rendered as saying not (as the German does say) that *one* of the formulas unites the other two in itself, but instead that *each* or *any* of the three formulas unites the other two. Abbott (1883), Beck (1959), Liddell (1971) Gregor (1996), and Bennett (2010) all make this mistake, and Allison (2011, p. 257) appears to be defending the mistranslation using the philosophical argument that the formulas must be equivalent. Only Paton (1948), Ellington (1981), and Wood (2002) correctly translate *die eine* as "the one"; and Gregor's translation has been corrected by Timmermann (2012). This is also the only *philosophically* defensible reading of Kant's statement. Kant never says of either FUL/FLN or FH that it unites the other two in itself. In this clause, Kant is not *equating* all three formulas. On the contrary, he is *singling out* FA/FRE, *distinguishing* the *complete* formula from the other two (partial or one-sided) formulas. The common mistranslation seems to rest on, and at the same time it offers (misleading and bogus) support for, the confused and mistaken idea that the three formulas are "equivalent."

about what a moral principle is *for*. We have seen that for Kant, *none* of the formulas is meant to provide us with a procedure for deciding what to do. Each has its own problems to solve. But *telling us what to do* is not the problem set for any of the formulas.

For Kant, I decide what to do by devising for myself a virtuous life that fulfills my moral vocation: complying with various strict duties and including among my ends many examples of the duties of virtue (my own perfection, the happiness of others). I act on the ends and maxims that belong to the kind of life I have chosen, and the kind of person I have made myself to be. A rule or criterion that told me what to do would relieve me of the responsibility for having a good character and exercising good judgment. We should not even *want* a principle that did that. Shame on those philosophers who assume it is the sole aim of moral philosophy to provide a principle that would do this to us!

FA/FRE, as the *complete formula* of the moral law, does give us a command of reason: *Follow maxims with legislative form – those whose universal obedience would constitute a realm of ends*. We then apply these maxims to particular cases using FUL/FLN as a canon of judgment. If taken in that way, we want to say that Kant's formulas *tell us what to do*, then they do so only in coopera-tion or systematic combination. Does that make them *equivalent*? If it does, then a catcher is equivalent to a pitcher and a hammer to a nail. But if to say the formulas are *equivalent* is to give an affirmative answer to the question: "Do the three (or five) formulas, considered separately and independently, tell us to do the same things?" then the question makes a false assumption. We can no more answer Yes or No to it than to such silly and meaningless questions as: "Has Pope Francis stopped beating his wife?" or "Is Barack and Michelle Obama's eldest son a gay Republican?"

The "universal formula." I end by raising a question to which I have no confident answer. After stating the system of formulas at G 4:436, Kant notes that there is a progression of them, as in the categories of quantity, from unity (universality: FUL/FLN) to plurality (of the many ends in themselves, FH) to totality (FA/FRE: the moral law as a complete and unified system). He then adds this remark:

But one does better in judging (*Beurteilung*) to proceed in accordance with the strict method and take as ground the universal formula of the categorical imperative: Act in accordance with that maxim which can at the same time make itself into a universal law. But if one wants at the same time to obtain access for the moral law, then it is very useful to take one and the same action through the three named concepts and thus, as far as may be done, to bring the action nearer to intuition. (G 4:436–437)

Is the "universal formula" to be identified with any of the five formulas we have been examining? Or is it a formula distinct from all of them? This last thought was proposed by Klaus Reich (1939). It has not found much favor. Most readers have assumed, without even thinking, that the universal formula is FUL, perhaps because they confuse the term 'universal formula' with the conventional name for FUL (a name never used by Kant). I've argued that we should identify the "universal formula" with FA (see Wood, 1999, pp. 187–190 and Wood 2008, pp. 82–84). My first (and principal) reason for this is that the formula commands that we act in accordance with a maxim that can at the same time *make itself* into a universal law. As I hope we can see from the above discussion, FA and FUL are different, and this is a statement of FA, not of FUL. A second reason is that in the sentence following the statement of the universal formula, Kant is clearly distinguishing between the more abstract and austere versions of the first and third formulas and the more intuitive versions, which have just been used in systematizing the law. He is plainly saying that for purposes of *judgment*, we should use the more austere formulas, not the more intuitive ones. The paragraph began with FRE, the more intuitive form of FA, which (as I hope the paragraphs at the end of §8 enable us to see) is also the most intuitively appealing formula of all. So it is reasonable to suppose him to be stating the more austere form of FRE, which is FA. FA is also the formula that "of itself unites the other two in itself," so in that sense too FA is the "universal formula."

But I can no longer be entirely comfortable with this conclusion either. For Kant says the universal formula is to be used for judgment (*Beurteilung*). That function, however, was assigned to FUL and FLN, never to FA. So how can he now be saying that in judging actions, we should always use FA? There is another puzzle about this claim as well. If Kant is saying that the more intuitive variants are not as well suited for judgment, then that seems inconsistent with his use of FLN (the intuitive version of FUL) in the examples at G 4:421–424 (see Note 8 above).

For these reasons, I must confess I am not certain what the "universal formula" is supposed to be. But I suspect this little puzzle will be the least of the perplexities the above account will produce in minds accustomed to the usual ways in which Kant has been commonly read (or rather, as I insist, *misread*). So I will end here and leave all the issues for them to think about.[32]

Sources

Kant's writings will be referred to according to the following system of abbreviations:

AA *Immanuel Kants Schriften.* Ausgabe der königlich preussischen Akademie der Wissenschaften (Berlin: W. de Gruyter, 1900–). Unless otherwise footnoted, writings of Immanuel Kant will be cited by volume:page number in this edition.

Ca *Cambridge Edition of the Writings of Immanuel Kant* (New York: Cambridge University Press, 1992–) This edition provides marginal Ak volume:page citations.

Anth *Anthropologie in pragmatischer Hinsicht* (1798), AA 7 *Anthropology from a pragmatic point of view*, Ca Anthropology, History, and Education

---

[32] The thoughts expressed in this essay have benefited from interactions with many people over many years. They include (but are not limited to): Henry Allison, Marcia Baron, Kyla Ebels-Duggan, Uri Eran, Marilia Espirito Santo, Paul Guyer, Barbara Herman, David Hills, Desmond Hogan, Shelly Kagan, Samuel Kahn, Anna Kessler, Pauline Kleingeld, Suzanne Love, Meica Magnani, Allen Rosen, Tamar Schapiro, Dieter Schönecker, Jens Timmermann, Ralph Wedgwood, and Howard Williams. I doubt that any of these people agrees with everything I have said here, but that doesn't mean I won't keep listening to them and also keep trying to convince them.

TPP   *Zum ewigen Frieden: Ein philosophischer Entwurf* (1795), AA 8
      Toward perpetual peace: A philosophical project, Ca Practical Philosophy

G   *Grundlegung zur Metaphysik der Sitten* (1785), AA 4
      Grundlegung zur Metaphysik der Sitten (1785, 1786), ed. Bernd Kraft and Dieter Schönecker (Hamburg: Felix Meiner Verlag, 1999).
      Groundwork of the metaphysics of morals, Ca Practical Philosophy
      Groundwork for the Metaphysics of Morals, trans. Allen Wood, second edition (New Haven: Yale University Press, 2018).

IUH   *Idee zu einer allgemeinen Geschichte in weltbürgerlicher Absicht* (1784), AA 8
      Idea toward a universal history with a cosmopolitan aim, Ca Anthropology, History, and Education

FI   Erste Einleitung der *Kritik der Urteilskraft,* AA 20
      First Introduction to the Critique of the Power of Judgment, Ca Critique of the Power of Judgment

CPR   *Kritik der reinen Vernunft* (1781, 1787). Cited by A/B pagination.
      Critique of pure reason, Ca Critique of Pure Reason

CPrR *Kritik der praktischen Vernunft* (1788), AA 5
      Critique of practical reason, Ca Practical Philosophy

CJ   *Kritik der Urteilskraft* (1790), AA 5
      Critique of the power of judgment, Ca Critique of the Power of Judgment

CB   *Mutmaßlicher Anfang der Menschengeschichte* (1786), AA 8
      Conjectural beginning of human history, Ca Anthropology, History, and Education

MM   *Metaphysik der Sitten* (1797–1798), AA 6
      Metaphysics of morals, Ca Practical Philosophy

WOT   *Was heißt: Sich im Denken orientieren?* (1786), AA 8
      What does it mean to orient oneself in thinking? Ca Religion and Rational Theology

P   *Prolegomena zu einer jeden künftigen Metaphysik* (1783),
           AA 4
           Prolegomena to Any Future Metaphysics, Ca Theoretical
           Philosophy after 1781
Rel   *Religion innerhalb der Grenzen der bloßen Vernunft*
           (1793–1794), AA 6
           Religion within the boundaries of mere reason, Ca Religion
           and Rational Theology
RH   *Recensionen von Herders Ideen zu der Philosophie der
           Geschichte der Menschheit,* Theil 1.-2, AA 8
           Reviews of Herder's Ideas for the Philosophy of History of
           Humanity, Ca Anthropology, History, and Education
TP   *Über den Gemeinspruch: Das mag in der Theorie richtig
           sein, taugt aber nicht für die Praxis* (1793), AA 8
           *On the common saying: That may be correct in theory but it
           is of no use in practice,* Ca Practical Philosophy
UTP   *Über den Gebrauch teleologischer Prinzipien in der
           Philosophie,* AA 8
           On the Use of Teleological Principles in Philosophy, Ca
           Anthropology, History, and Education
L-Eth   *Vorlesungen über Ethik,* AA 27, 29
           Lectures on Ethics, Ca Lectures on Ethics
WIE   *Beantwortung der Frage: Was ist Aufklärung?* (1784), AA 8
           An answer to the question: What is enlightenment? Ca
           Practical Philosophy

Other sources

Allison, Henry (2011). *Kant's Groundwork for the Metaphysics of Morals:
   A Commentary.* Oxford: Oxford University Press.
Aristotle (1999). *Nicomachean Ethics,* 2nd edn., trans. Terence Irwin.
   Indianapolis: Hackett. Abbreviated 'NE' and cited by Becker number.
Baron, Marcia (1991). "Impartiality and Friendship," *Ethics* 101, 836–857.
Brucker, Johann Jacob (1742–1744). *Historia Critica Philosophiae a mundi
   incunabulis ad nostrum aetatum deducta,* 5 vols. Leipzig: Weidemann
   and Reich, Pars II, Cap. II, Lib. VII.

Dworkin, Ronald (2011). *Justice for Hedgehogs.* Cambridge, MA: Harvard University Press.

Fahmy, Melissa Seymour (2009). "Active Sympathetic Participation: Reconsidering Kant's Duty of Sympathy," *Kantian Review* 14(1), 31–52.

Fichte, Johann Gottlieb (2011). *Attempt at a Critique of All Revelation*, trans. Garrett Green, ed. A. Wood. Cambridge: Cambridge University Press.

Greene, Joshua (2008). "The Secret Joke of Kant's Soul," in W. Sinnott-Armstrong (ed.), *Moral Psychology*, Volume 3. Cambridge, MA: MIT Press.

Guyer, Paul (2014 [2006]). *Kant.* London: Routledge.

Hegel, G. W. F. (1991). *Elements of the Philosophy of Right*, trans. H. B. Nisbet, ed. A. Wood, Cambridge: Cambridge University Press.

Herman, Barbara (1993). *The Practice of Moral Judgment.* Cambridge, MA: Harvard University Press.

Hume, David (2005 [1783]). *Of Suicide.* New York: Penguin.

Kaufman, Alexander (1996). *Welfare in the Kantian State.* Oxford: Clarendon Press.

Kleingeld, Pauline (2017). "Contradiction and Kant's Formula of Universal Law," in E. Watkins (ed.), *Kant, Agency and Persons.* Cambridge: Cambridge University Press.

Korsgaard, Christine (1996a). *Creating the Kingdom of Ends.* Cambridge: Cambridge University Press.

Korsgaard, Christine (1996b). *The Sources of Normativity*, ed. Onora O'Neill. Cambridge: Cambridge University Press.

Korsgaard, Christine (2009). *Self-Constitution.* Oxford: Oxford University Press.

Lyons, David B. (1965). *The Forms and Limits of Utilitarianism.* Oxford: Clarendon Press.

Mill, John Stuart (2001). *Utilitarianism*, 2nd edn., ed. George Sher. Indianapolis: Hackett.

Mossner, Ernest Campbell (1970). *The Life of David Hume.* Oxford: Oxford University Press.

Nietzsche, Friedrich (2002). *Beyond Good and Evil: Prelude to the Philosophy of the Future*, ed. Rolf-Peter Horstmann and Judith Norman. Cambridge: Cambridge University Press.

O'Neill, Onora (1989). *Constructions of Reason: Explorations of Kant's Practical Philosophy.* Cambridge: Cambridge University Press.

O'Neill, Onora (2013). *Acting on Principle: An Essay in Kantian Ethics*, 2nd edn. Cambridge: Cambridge University Press. First edition: New York: Columbia University Press, 1975.

Rawls, John. (1989). "Themes in Kant's Moral Philosophy," in E. Förster (ed.), *Kant's Transcendental Deductions*. Stanford, CA: Stanford University Press.

Rawls, John (2000). *Lectures on the History of Moral Philosophy*, ed. Barbara Herman. Cambridge, MA: Harvard University Press.

Reich, Klaus (1939). "Kant and Greek Ethics I–II," trans W. H. Walsh. *Mind* 48, 338–354.

Rivera-Castro, Faviola (2014). "Kant's Formula of the Universal Law of Nature Reconsidered," *Journal of Moral Philosophy* 11(2), 185–208.

Sade, Marquis de (1966 [1791]). *Justine, Philosophy in the Bedroom, and other writings*, trans. R. Seaver and A. Wainhouse. New York: Grove Press.

Scheffler, Samuel (1992). *Human Morality*. Oxford: Oxford University Press.

Schönecker, Dieter and Allen Wood (2015). *Immanuel Kant's Groundwork for the Metaphysics of Morals: A Commentary*. Cambridge, MA: Harvard University Press.

Timmermann, Jens (2007). *Kant's Groundwork of the Metaphysics of Morals: A Commentary*. Cambridge: Cambridge University Press.

Tittel, Gottlob August (2012 [1786]). *Über Herrn Kants Moralreform*. Charleston, SC: Nabu Press.

Williams, Bernard (1981). *Moral Luck*. Cambridge: Cambridge University Press.

Wolf, Susan (2003). "'One Thought Too Many': Love, Morality, and the Ordering of Commitment," in Ulrike Heuer and Gerald Land (eds.), *Luck, Value, and Commitment: Themes from the Ethics of Bernard Williams*. Oxford: Oxford University Press

Wolff, Robert Paul (1972). *The Autonomy of Reason*. New York: Harper & Row.

Wood, Allen (1990). *Hegel's Ethical Thought*. New York: Cambridge University Press.

Wood, Allen (1999). *Kant's Ethical Thought*. New York: Cambridge University Press.

Wood, Allen (2001). "The Moral Law as a System of Formulas," in H. Stolzenberg and H. F. Fulda (eds.), *Architektonik und System in der Philosophie Kants*. Hamburg: Meiner Verlag.

Wood, Allen (2008). *Kantian Ethics*. New York: Cambridge University Press.

Wood, Allen (2014). *The Free Development of Each: Studies in Freedom, Right and Ethics in Classical German Philosophy*. Oxford: Oxford University Press.

Wood, Allen (2016). *Fichte's Ethical Thought*. Oxford: Oxford University Press.

Wood, Allen (2017a). "Kant on Friendship," in Oliver Sensen and Stefano Bacin (eds.), *Kant's Ethics in Context*. Cambridge: Cambridge University Press.

Wood, Allen (2017b). "Universal Law," in E. Watkins (ed.), *Kant, Agency and Persons*. Cambridge: Cambridge University Press.

Printed in the United States
By Bookmasters